THE STUDENT EQ EDGE

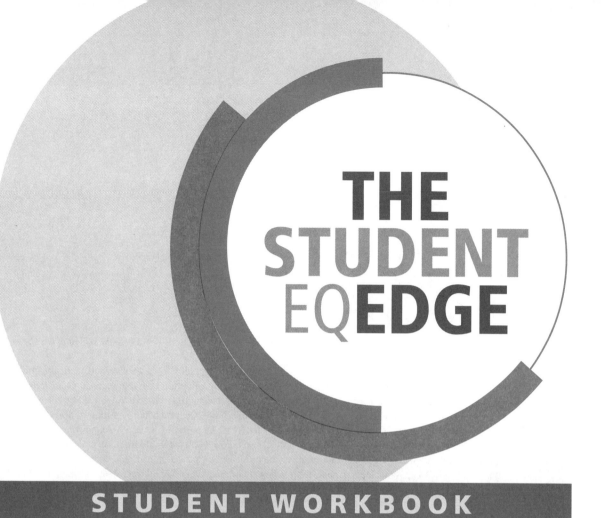

THE STUDENT EQEDGE

STUDENT WORKBOOK

Korrel Kanoy • Howard E. Book • Steven J. Stein

JOSSEY-BASS
A Wiley Imprint
www.josseybass.com

Jossey-Bass books and products are available through most bookstores. To contact Jossey-Bass directly call our Customer Care Department within the U.S. at 800-956-7739, outside the U.S. at 317-572-3986, or fax 317-572-4002.

Wiley publishes in a variety of print and electronic formats and by print-on-demand. Some material included with standard print versions of this book may not be included in e-books or in print-on-demand. If this book refers to media such as a CD or DVD that is not included in the version you purchased, you may download this material at http://booksupport.wiley.com. For more information about Wiley products, visit www.wiley.com.

ISBN: 9781118094600

Printed in the United States of America
FIRST EDITION

PB PRINTING   10 9 8 7 6 5 4 3 2 1

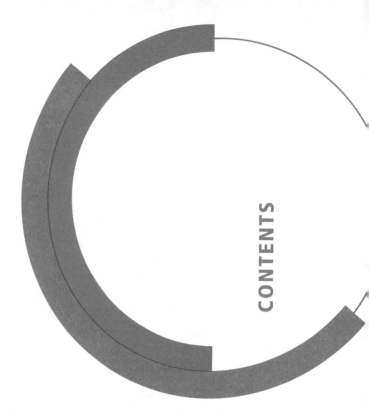

CONTENTS

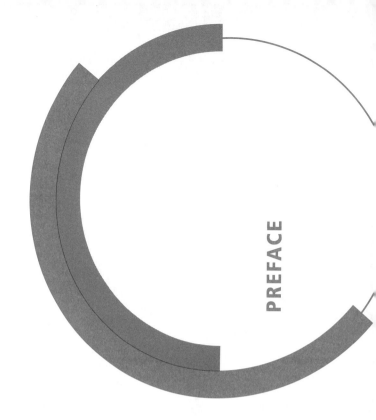

One of the authors, Korrel, taught at the college and university level for over 30 years and quickly learned that students rarely read the preface, so we'll keep this one very short!

There are many reasons (better grades, increased chances of graduating, better career performance) why you may want to take this workbook very seriously. Do the exercises, read more about emotional intelligence in *The Student EQ Edge: Emotional Intelligence and Your Academic and Personal Success* (Stein, Book, & Kanoy, 2013), and practice your new skills. If you do so, you will reap many rewards in your educational, professional, and personal life.

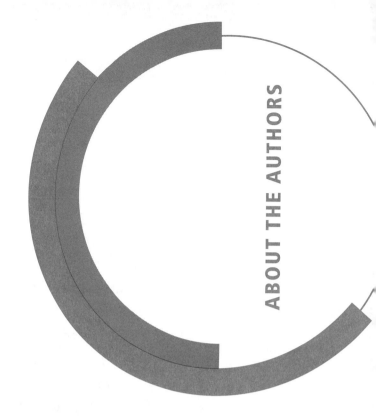

Korrel Kanoy, Ph.D., is a developmental psychologist and served as a professor of psychology at William Peace University for over 30 years, where she won the McCormick Distinguished Teaching Award and the Excellence in Campus Leadership Award. She has taught college-level courses in emotional intelligence since 1998. Korrel designed a comprehensive approach to infusing emotional intelligence into first-year experience courses, disciplinary senior capstone courses, and college and university service offices. She has worked with over 200 college students to help them develop emotional intelligence and has worked with schools to hire the best teachers using emotional intelligence as part of the hiring process. She has published a children's book, *Annie's Lost Hat,* which teaches preschoolers lessons about emotional intelligence through the story. She is a coauthor of *Building Leadership Skills in Adolescent Girls.*

 Steven J. Stein, Ph.D., is a psychologist and CEO of Multi-Health Systems (MHS), a leading international test publishing company. He has authored several books on emotional intelligence, including the original *The EQ Edge: Emotional Intelligence and Your Success* (coauthored with Dr. Howard Book); *Make Your Workplace Great: The Seven Keys to an Emotionally Intelligent Organization*; and *Emotional Intelligence for Dummies.* He has given presentations on emotional intelligence to audiences throughout the United States, Canada, Mexico, Europe, Asia, and Africa. As well, he has appeared on hundreds of TV, radio, online, and print media productions.

For over a dozen years, **Dr. Howard E. Book**'s area of expertise has been benchmarking and enhancing the emotional intelligence of individuals and groups, as well as developing training programs to enhance the strength of this ability. Dr. Book has also written, lectured, and offered workshops on the importance of emotional intelligence and success in the real world internationally. He is a member of the Consortium for Research in Emotional Intelligence in Organizations, part-time faculty at the INSEAD School of Business in France and Singapore, and a former board member of the International Society for the Psychoanalytic Study of Organizations, and with Dr. Steven Stein he coauthored the book *The EQ Edge: Emotional Intelligence and Your Success*. He holds the rank of associate professor, Department of Psychiatry, Faculty of Medicine, at the University of Toronto.

Chapter 1

Introduction to Emotional Intelligence

Most of us grew up with a limited view of what it meant to be intelligent. We thought about those tests they gave us in school at the end of the year and the grades we earned. We thought about vocabulary words or math skills or reading comprehension. We took for granted that intelligence was important. And it is. We knew what IQ was about. But what about EQ? Emotional quotient, or EQ, is a measure of another form of intelligence. Intelligence is broader than we once thought and extends far beyond book learning or innate ability; it includes how we understand and use our emotions and relate to others to produce positive outcomes. The more we learn about emotional intelligence or EI (which is what EQ measures), the more we understand that well-developed EI may predict our future success and satisfaction better than our "book" intelligence or grades in school. Chapter 19 in *The Student EQ Edge: Emotional Intelligence and Your Academic and Personal Success* (Stein, Book, & Kanoy, 2013) outlines the many benefits of EI to students in academic settings. And the influence of EI is equally important in predicting our personal and professional success.

Maybe you already knew how important EI is and that's why you're taking this class or participating in this workshop. Or maybe it's a requirement. Either way, if you are motivated (that in itself is a form of EI!), willing to adapt your behavior based on what you learn (again, another EI skill), and participate fully in all the leader asks (another EI-related ability), you will benefit. How? Here's one example. Schulman (1995) found that the EI skill of optimism was a better predictor of first-year students' college GPA than their SAT scores. And in a dissertation project involving 783 college students studied over a five-year period, Sparkman (2009) found the following:

- Social responsibility, impulse control, and empathy (all EI skills) were the three strongest positive predictors of college graduation.
- Self-actualization, social responsibility, and happiness (all EI skills) were positive predictors of cumulative GPA, but very high independence and interpersonal relationship skills were negative predictors of cumulative GPA (more about that later).

Finally, many employers seek graduates who can work well independently and in teams, control stress, solve problems, change directions when necessary, and relate well both to coworkers and customers. In fact, Shivpuri and Kim (2004) found that employers ranked interpersonal skills as the number one skill they wanted students to possess!

Emotional Intelligence Overview

EI is "a set of emotional and social skills that influence the way we perceive and express ourselves, develop and maintain social relationships, cope with challenges, and use emotional information in an effective and meaningful way" (*The EQ Edge*, 2011, p. 13). Figure 1.1 shows the five realms and sixteen scales of EI. Consult *The Student EQ Edge: Emotional Intelligence and Your Academic and Personal Success*

Figure 1.1 Emotional Intelligence Defined

SELF-PERCEPTION

Self-Regard is respecting oneself while understanding and accepting one's strength and weaknesses. Self-Regard is often associated with feelings of inner strength and self-confidence.

Self-Actualization is the willingness to persistently try to improve oneself and engage in the pursuit of personally relevant and meaningful objectives that lead to a rich and enjoyable life.

Emotional Self-Awareness includes recognizing and understanding one's own emotions. This includes the ability to differentiate between subtleties in one's own emotions while understanding the cause of these emotions and the impact they have on the thoughts and actions of oneself and others.

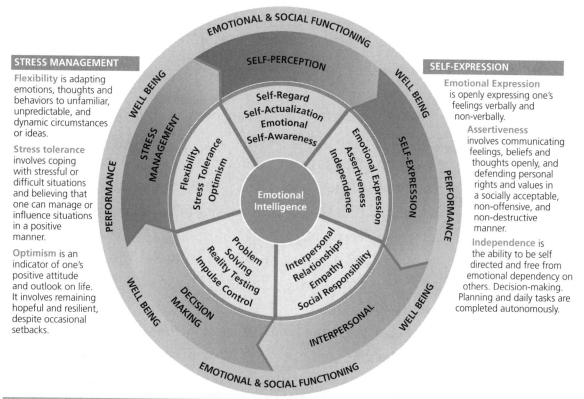

STRESS MANAGEMENT

Flexibility is adapting emotions, thoughts and behaviors to unfamiliar, unpredictable, and dynamic circumstances or ideas.

Stress tolerance involves coping with stressful or difficult situations and believing that one can manage or influence situations in a positive manner.

Optimism is an indicator of one's positive attitude and outlook on life. It involves remaining hopeful and resilient, despite occasional setbacks.

SELF-EXPRESSION

Emotional Expression is openly expressing one's feelings verbally and non-verbally.

Assertiveness involves communicating feelings, beliefs and thoughts openly, and defending personal rights and values in a socially acceptable, non-offensive, and non-destructive manner.

Independence is the ability to be self directed and free from emotional dependency on others. Decision-making. Planning and daily tasks are completed autonomously.

DECISION MAKING

Problem Solving is the ability to find solutions to problems in situations where emotions are involved. Problem solving includes the ability to understand how emotions impact decision making.

Reality Testing is the capacity to remain objective by seeing things as they really are. This capacity involves recognizing when emotions or personal bias can cause one to be less objective.

Impulse Control is the ability to resist or delay an impulse, drive or temptation to act and involves avoiding rash behaviors and decision making.

INTERPERSONAL

Interpersonal Relationships refers to the skill of developing and maintaining mutually satisfying relationships that are characterized by trust and compassion.

Empathy is recognizing, understanding and appreciating how other people feel. Empathy involves being able to articulate your understanding of another's perspective and behaving in a way that respects other' feelings.

Social Responsibility is willingly contributing to society, to one's social groups, and generally to the welfare of others. Social Responsibility involves acting responsibly, having social consciousness, and showing concern for the greater community.

(Stein, Book, & Kanoy, 2013) for additional information about each scale.

We assume you'd like to make good grades, have meaningful and healthy relationships, and graduate and begin your career. Developing your EI will help you accomplish those goals. So let's get started!

A Word About EI Scales and Skills

The model of EI presented in *The Student EQ Edge: Emotional Intelligence and Your Academic and Personal Success* and in this companion workbook identifies 16 scales. You can also think of these scales as *skills you can develop.* For example, assertiveness is both a scale in the EQ-i 2.0 model and a skill you can develop.

The Student EQ Edge: Student Workbook: An Overview

This workbook serves as a companion piece to *The Student EQ Edge: Emotional Intelligence and Your Academic and Personal Success* and thus covers the same EI scales in the same order. The workbook will help you to gain a better understanding of the EI scales, reflect about your behavior in those areas, and practice some skill development.

Chapter 2 provides you with case studies; observing others' behavior makes it easier to identify how important EI is in our daily lives.

Self-Perception—In Chapters 3–5 you will gain a greater understanding of who you are, your strengths and limitations, how you process and reflect about your emotions, and how well you have identified meaningful goals and activities for your life.

Self-Expression—Chapters 6–8 will help you understand how effectively you express your emotions, whether you can be appropriately independent in various situations, and how assertive you are.

Interpersonal Relationship—Chapters 9–11 will help you understand how well you connect with others, how well you understand and connect with others' emotions, and how much you try to contribute and cooperate to make things better for everyone.

Decision Making—Chapters 12–14 cover your decision-making skills. How well do you assess the facts in a situation without over- or underemphasizing them? How do your emotions affect the way you view situations and how you problem solve? Do you problem solve effectively when you are emotionally charged? And can you maintain control over your impulses in a variety of situations so that you think before acting?

Stress Management: Chapters 15–17 will help you understand how well you cope with stress. Are you able to remain internally calm and focused when stressed out? Are you able to change your behavior when circumstances change, or does change stress you out? Do you remain optimistic even when you confront obstacles?

Well-Being: Chapter 18 examines your happiness and overall well-being and how that is influenced by some of the topics covered earlier.

Why Reflection?

Each activity ends with some questions that will help you reflect about what you have learned. Reflection improves academic performance and can be graded based on the depth of your analysis and the quality of your insights. High-quality reflection will help your course grade, but even more important, it will help *you!*

Consider three possible responses to a question that appears in Chapter 3 of this workbook: "What concerns do you have about developing emotional self-awareness?"

Sarah: "None; I think it will be fun. I love doing exercises and finding out more about myself. It's always interesting to see how I compare to other students."

Carlos: "I don't like talking about my feelings. My girlfriend always wants me to do more of that. I don't understand what the big deal is about emotions."

Aisha: "I sometimes find it hard to talk about my feelings. But if I become more aware of my feelings and what causes them, maybe I'll feel more comfortable talking about them."

Even though the lengths of the three answers are not different, their depth of reflection is very different. The first student talks only about how much she enjoys exercises. She's dodged the question. Carlos starts off with some reflection but then ends his statement by challenging the notion that it's an important question to consider. Aisha, on the other hand, takes stock of her emotions and behavior and reflects effectively about how things might change. Reflections don't have to be long or even too personal, but effective reflection will help you understand yourself better, ultimately leading to better outcomes.

Case Studies of Emotionally Intelligent (and Not Emotionally Intelligent!) Behavior

It's always easier to recognize how *others* mess things up or what they could have done differently to make a situation better. The case studies in this workbook are based on everyday challenges faced by students or young professionals. Although the scenarios and names are hypothetical, you will probably be able to identify similar situations in your life. Training yourself to think about how EI relates to a situation and coming up with solutions is the first step to improving your own emotional intelligence.

CASE STUDY #1: WHY CAN'T I MAKE AN A?

Briana just found out she made a B on a paper and her two friends made A's. She understands the professor's comments and knows that her writing is improving and needs to improve more, but she still can't shake the negative feelings she's having. When

7

her friends ask what grade she got, she doesn't want to discuss it with them. And she doesn't like hearing how happy they are about their A grades. Later, in math class, she begins thinking about the paper and misses an important formula explanation. She's too embarrassed to ask the faculty member to repeat the information. After classes that day, another friend approaches her and asks if she wants to go to shopping. Briana declines the invitation and instead goes to her room, puts on her headphones, and listens to her favorite music. Later that evening she attempts her math homework, but she struggles to work problems using the formula covered in class earlier that day. After a few minutes, she closes her book and goes to bed. She's restless, though, and it takes her a long time to go to sleep.

Reflection Questions

1. Citing information from the case study, identify what emotional intelligence skills are most relevant to this case study.

2. What values or hot buttons may have been activated when Briana found out she made a B on her paper? Do you think these same values or hot buttons would have been triggered if her friends had also made Bs?

3. How does Briana's emotional reaction affect her behaviors throughout the rest of the day? Is her behavior more or less productive the rest of the day? Explain your response.

● CASE STUDY #2: 15 YEARS TO GRADUATE

Jane was a 32-year-old woman with three kids ages 10, 9, and 5. She had dropped out of college at age 20 to marry her long-time boyfriend; since having her children she had worked part-time in administrative assistant positions. She was bored with these positions and wanted a bigger challenge and more money. Her husband, Mark, was a college graduate and worked as an accountant. He supported her decision and was eager to take on a larger role at home.

Jane enrolled in a nearby institution that offered degree-completion programs for adult learners. The week before classes began, Jane told her husband she didn't want to go back to school after all. When he gently probed for what had changed her mind, she replied, "What was I thinking? When will I have time to study? I've forgotten the math I learned, and I haven't written a paper in 12 years. What if I don't do well?"

After a lengthy conversation, Jane decided to give it a try. She could always drop out if her fears were realized.

The first month was very challenging. Jane frequently felt nervous, especially when she had to take a test or turn in an assignment. She came home every night exhausted and thinking about quitting. She couldn't find time to study as much as she thought she needed to. But she told herself that this was a big transition and she should give it some time.

Soon she developed a routine of studying while the kids were doing their homework, and she stayed on campus between her classes to study instead of racing home to do laundry. She and Mark developed a chore list for each kid so that everyone took on more responsibility at home. Studying with her kids while they did homework relieved some of her guilt because she could stop what she was doing to provide help if they needed it.

Two years later, Jane graduated with a degree in psychology. She was accepted to a master's program in counseling, and her goal was to open a business to work with adults who are making a mid-life transition.

Reflection Questions

1. Describe how Jane's self-perception changed from the time she entered to the time she graduated.
2. What EI skill(s) did her husband demonstrate?
3. What were Jane's biggest challenges, and how did she use EI to help overcome them?

CASE STUDY #3: BUT I'M GOOD!

Roberto is an average student but a very good athlete. His sisters both make all A's in their classes while he makes mostly C's and B's. But that's okay with Roberto because he excels at soccer. He starred on his high school team in his small hometown and earned a scholarship to play on a college team.

The first day of college practice did not go well. Roberto was surprised by how fast and strong everyone was. He got beaten badly on several plays, and the coach called him aside to give him pointers about his positioning and footwork. He vaguely remembered his high school coach saying some of the same things, but he hadn't paid attention then because he was playing so well.

Roberto didn't make the changes the coach suggested because what he had always done had worked great so far and this new coach didn't know him very well. Over the next several weeks, the coach kept emphasizing the same points to him and not offering him any encouragement or praise. Roberto began to get frustrated, but he kept his frustrations to himself. The coach just needed more time to understand his style of play.

During the first game of the season, Roberto started the game. But after he got caught out of position and the other team scored a goal, the coach took him out. Roberto sat on the bench and fumed. Everybody made mistakes—why did he get benched when others did not?

The same pattern continued for several weeks. During the fifth game of the season, Roberto played only the last couple of minutes, after his team had a 4–0 lead. Later that night, when talking to his parents, he told them he was thinking about quitting the team. He heard himself say, "I just don't think I'm good enough to play at the college level."

Reflection Questions

1. Citing information from the case study, identify which emotional intelligence skills are most relevant to this case study.

2. Was Roberto aware of his soccer weaknesses? What about his EI weaknesses? Explain.

3. Do you agree with Roberto's thoughts about quitting the team? Explain your answer.

CASE STUDY #4: STARTING COLLEGE

Jerome and Chris are first-year college students and roommates, and it's the first time either has lived away from home. Jerome has declared a major in premed; he signed up for a heavy academic load this semester and has two science classes with labs. He spends lots of time in the library, and at the end of the first semester he has a 3.5 GPA. Jerome likes to go out on the weekends and have fun and often attends sports events or parties. He has lots of friends and is adjusting well to college. He sometimes gets bored when reading or studying, but if he does, he takes a short break to play video games.

Chris came to the university without a major and remains "undeclared" at the beginning of second semester. He doesn't see a need to rush to declare a major, so he did not take a class in Career Exploration that his faculty advisor recommended. Chris made good grades in high school but is finding it harder to attend college classes without his parents around to make sure that he gets up on time. He's asked Jerome to make sure he gets up in the morning and goes to class, but occasionally he goes back to sleep after Jerome wakes him up. Chris tends to study right before a test by staying up all night. He goes out a lot during the week and plays every intramural sport offered. Chris made a 2.2 GPA first semester. He's surprised he did not do better because he was such a good student in high school.

Reflection Questions

1. Citing information from the case study, identify what emotional intelligence skills are most relevant to this case study.

2. Which student are you more similar to right now? What is your motivation for academic work? If you don't see yourself as similar to either of these students, where do you see yourself on the continuum from not knowing what you want to study to being absolutely sure what you want to study? Explain.

3. Many college students do not declare a major during their first year of college. In that case, what could students do to ensure that they stay on track and motivated?

CASE STUDY #5: SHARED RESPONSIBILITIES

Keandra was a resident assistant (RA) in a college dorm. The other RA, Ian, had been relying on Keandra to file all of the reports and paperwork instead of the two of them taking turns as they agreed to do at the beginning of the year. The reports have deadlines, and if they are not turned in on time, the RAs could be fired.

Keandra went up to Ian's room one afternoon and brought up the paperwork issue. Here's their conversation.

Keandra: "There's been a lot of paperwork lately. You need to do your part of it."

Ian: "I'm not very good at paperwork."

Keandra: "Maybe so, but you took the job knowing that was part of what you had to do."

Ian: "Well, I have a heavier course load than you do. Can't you just keep doing it this semester?"

Keandra: "I have a heavy load too. We both get paid the same amount, and I'm doing a lot more of the work than you are."

Ian (in irritated tone): "I don't have time for this discussion." Ian walks out of the room.

Reflection Questions

1. What emotional intelligence dimensions are relevant to this interaction? Cite examples from the scenario to support your opinion.

2. What should Keandra do next? What EI skills can she draw on to help her resolve this issue?

3. Compare how you typically handle a situation in which someone is trying to take advantage of you to how Keandra handled this situation.

CASE STUDY #6: A COSTLY DECISION

James was a junior in college with a 3.3 GPA who was taking 12 credit hours for the semester. He missed the first several classes of a one-credit hour course. He emailed the financial aid office to ask whether he would be considered a full-time student if he audited the class instead of taking it for a grade. They responded that audits don't count toward total hours, so he would be considered a part-time student with just 11 credit hours if he audited the class. James then assumed that if he dropped the class he would lose his financial aid and have to pay for his classes. James knew he could not pay his tuition, so he decided to stay in the class, but he never attended again and did not complete any of the assignments. Nor did he contact the professor.

One day the professor saw James on campus and offered to help him complete the coursework through an independent study. James was on his way to look at the latest iPad when he ran into the professor, so he thanked the professor and asked if he could come by the professor's office the next day.

The next day James had to work on a major term paper. He was so tired the following day from pulling an all-nighter that he went to sleep as soon as he turned his paper in. One week later he remembered the professor's offer, but he was sure the professor wouldn't still let him do an independent study. James never went to talk with the professor, and ultimately he earned an F in the course, which hurt his overall GPA.

The Reality (facts about financial aid at James's school)

- At James's institution, students are allowed a one-time exception to go below 12 credit hours during one semester and not lose any current or future financial aid. James has never used this exception.

- James was given the information about the one-time exception for going below 12 hours when he received financial aid, but he did not consult this information when the situation occurred.
- An Independent Study option would have been available through the first six weeks of the following semester with the professor's agreement.

Reflection Questions

1. What questions should James have asked the financial aid office that he did not ask?
2. What difference would these questions have made in this situation?
3. What emotional intelligence challenges does James face?

CASE STUDY #7: FIRST JOB JITTERS

Stacey completed her college degree in December and was hired by a major accounting firm to help them with their caseload during tax season. January involved lots of meetings with clients and getting to know her colleagues. Up to this point, Stacey loved her job.

In February the workload picked up, and Stacey was given several tax returns to complete that she thought were very difficult. She checked in frequently with a senior partner about whether she was doing things correctly. He always praised the quality of her work. One day the senior partner remarked that she was a better accountant than she gave herself credit for. Still, she sought his advice a lot.

At the beginning of March, she noticed that the partner was keeping his door closed more often now, and she was scared to interrupt him. So she asked one of the other new hires to look over her work. As the caseload built, Stacey got farther and farther behind. She carefully checked and rechecked every return before submitting it because she knew it would look bad if she made errors. She stopped doing yoga and going for weekend runs and used that time to catch up on work. Even though she was spending more time at work, it was taking her longer and longer to get each tax return done. One day, after Stacey complained to an administrative assistant (AA) that she had not known how hard tax season would be, the AA told her to "get a grip." Stacey fled to her office in tears.

By March 25, Stacey didn't see how she could make it through another three weeks. When she woke up that morning, she decided to quit her job. She called the office and told the senior partner she was resigning. He asked her to reconsider, citing the fact that her work was quite good and that she had 30 returns she needed to complete in the next three weeks. There was no way anyone else in the firm could take on more work, he said, and they were counting on her.

Stacey held firm and said no. She felt really bad about it at first, but as the day went on she felt better. She went to her yoga class, then went shopping and spent $400 on new clothes she would need for interviewing with other companies.

Reflection Questions

1. What EI characteristics are evident in this case study? Cite examples from the case to support your choices.
2. Which one or two EI areas were most problematic for Stacey in this case study?
3. Do you agree with Stacey's decision to quit? Why or why not?

CASE STUDY #8: NO WAY

After child development class one day, Professor Tripp said, "Chloe, I think you should consider going on this international study trip this summer with me. You'll get to visit five different countries, learn about other cultures, and earn three credit hours."

Chloe responded, "No way."

The professor inquired why not, and Chloe remarked that she couldn't stand to travel because she liked things "just so" and travel disrupted that.

The professor replied, "Well, you told me at the beginning of this child development class you want to have kids one day. You can't always control what happens next when you have kids."

Chloe looked stunned. She had been learning about children's development but had not yet connected that to how she would have to adapt her life. So she decided to go on the trip.

The first few days of the trip, usually the most exciting for students, were horrible for Chloe. She hated the fact that each day brought a different schedule; she didn't eat well because the food was different; and she clung close to the professors whenever the group had to take the Tube, the London subway system. She refused invitations from other students unless one of the professors was going with the group. The thought of accidentally getting separated from the group was a constant concern for her.

As the days passed and nothing horrible happened, Chloe began to relax a little. By the end of the first week she was experimenting with new foods, going off with other students to explore the city during free time, and beginning to have a good time. By the end of the second week, Chloe had emerged as a group leader. She planned evening outings for the students (sans the professors!) and was always among the first to master the public transportation system of a new city. The transformation was incredible.

Her reflection paper at the end of the travel experience concluded with a simple but telling self-assessment: "I always feared change because I liked my life the way it was; I had no idea that change could be so exciting and freeing. Also, I had no idea how much I would benefit in other ways. I feel more confident in myself and more equipped to handle things that may happen to me as an adult."

Reflection Questions

1. What were Chloe's biggest challenges in terms of emotional intelligence?
2. What areas of emotional intelligence were the most positively affected by Chloe's willingness to take this trip? Explain how she improved in each area.

● CASE STUDY #9: TWINS?

Maria and Lupe are fraternal twins. They grew up together in Mexico and moved to the United States when they were fourteen. They started high school that fall after living in the United States for only a month. Although they both had studied English in school, speaking it every day and writing papers in English was very difficult. They confronted other challenges, such as forming new friendships at their high school and finding interests they could pursue.

One day in the school cafeteria, they were approached by a popular girl named Emma, who invited them to go to the Friday night football game with them. Maria eagerly accepted for both of them.

After Emma left, Lupe told Maria how upset she was that Maria had agreed for them to go to the game. She wondered what they would talk about, how they would fit in with Emma's group of friends, and whether they would be made fun of because of their noticeable accents. Maria, on the other hand, expressed excitement about going. She tried to convince Lupe that this was a great opportunity to make new friends, to get involved at their new school, and to do something on Friday night other than stay home.

As Friday night approached, Maria's excitement grew, but so did Lupe's anxiety. Lupe could hardly pay attention in any of her classes that Friday as she thought about all the things that might happen that night. She worried about what to wear, how they would find Emma and her friends in the crowd of people at the game, and what she could talk about. She ate little of her lunch, and by the time school was over, she told Maria she didn't want to go that night.

Maria couldn't believe what Lupe was saying. This was their big chance to make some new friends! She had gone online to find pictures of previous football games, and she knew what to wear. She had also texted Emma and found a place to meet at the game. Yes, she was nervous, but she knew she would find things to talk about once she got to the game. She finally talked Lupe into going.

As their parents drove them to the game, Maria's excitement grew. She chatted with her mom while Lupe sat quietly, thinking of the many things that could go wrong and how embarrassed she would be. When her parents stopped the car to let the girls out, Lupe turned to Maria and blurted out, "I'm not going."

Maria was stunned. She tried to talk Lupe into changing her mind, but Lupe wouldn't budge. Maria finally turned to her parents and asked, "Can I go alone?" Her parents agreed if she would text them after connecting with Emma.

Maria got out of the car, made her way through the crowd, and finally saw Emma and her friends near the entrance. She was still nervous but glad she had come.

After a night filled with watching an exciting game and talking with Emma and her friends about music, clothes, and everything happening at school, Maria felt terrific. By the end of the night, she couldn't wait to see everyone again at school on Monday.

Reflection Questions

1. What emotional intelligence areas are most evident in the Twins case study?
2. Emotional intelligence involves, among other things, managing our emotions and effectively managing our relationships with others. How are those evident in this scenario?
3. Lupe obviously felt strong anxiety, and most people cannot just tell themselves to calm down or to quit worrying. What can you do in such a situation to help yourself?

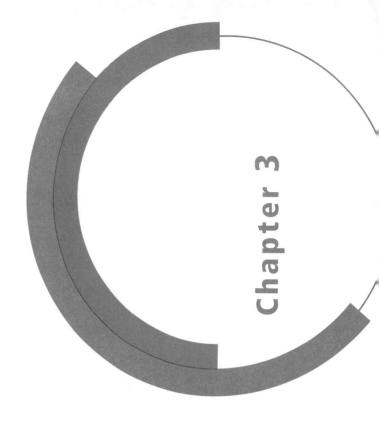

Chapter 3

Emotional Self-Awareness

Emotional self-awareness is the ability to recognize your feelings, differentiate between them, know why you are feeling these feelings, and recognize the impact your feelings have on others around you.
—Stein and Book, 2011, p. 53

What is emotional self-awareness? The ancient Greek aphorism (saying) "Know thyself" sums up emotional self-awareness. If you can become aware of your emotions as they happen, understand the reasons behind your emotions, and then understand the impact your emotions have on your behavior and how you interact with others, you will be happier and more productive, and have more meaningful relationships.

Sound challenging? It is, so keep reading!

Why Emotional Self-Awareness?

All of us have had it happen. We're feeling vaguely excited or somewhat down but cannot pinpoint an exact cause. Or we're feeling slightly anxious but without a tangible reason we can identify. Or we know what triggered our emotion but cannot figure out why we reacted as we did. If you understand what causes your emotions, you have the opportunity to either change your emotional reactions to events (for example, become less anxious about writing a big paper) or change your behavioral reactions (for example, stop procrastinating because you are anxious). Emotional self-awareness also enables you to understand why you reacted positively and productively to certain situations, increasing the chances you'll do so again. For example, Andre realized the vague directions from his teacher had confused him and made him not want to work on his project. So he asked for clarification and then became excited about his idea for the project and did well.

Behaviors That Demonstrate Effective Emotional Self-Awareness

- You use emotion words such as *mad, sad, scared, frustrated.*
- You are aware when your mood or emotion changes.
- You can identify the cause or reason for an emotional shift.
- You observe others for their reactions to your emotions.

Behaviors That Demonstrate a Lack of Emotional Self-Awareness

- Ignoring your feelings or pretending they don't exist.
- Refusing to reflect about things that have happened to you and how you responded.
- Making fun of emotions in yourself and others instead of understanding their impact.

Worksheet 3.1: Feelings Journal

Name:

At least three times per day on four different days, fill in the following form to chart your feelings. Some examples are provided to help you get started.

Date	Location	Feeling	Possible triggers
1/11	Class	Anxious	Professor announced a test next week
1/11	Cafeteria	Calmer	Joe asked if we could study together for the test
1/11	Hallway	Excited	Got asked to a party Friday night
1/11	Class	Proud	Professor quoted from my paper in class

Reflection Questions

1. Count the number of positive and negative emotions and then divide positive/negative. By definition, every emotion is either positive or negative, so classify each one! If you experience more positive emotions, your final number will be higher than one; if more negative, less than one.
   a. What is your ratio of positive to negative emotions?
   b. How do you think this affects you throughout your day?
2. What other patterns do you see in your journal? Look for types of situations or certain people that trigger similar emotions and explain what you find.
3. Which emotions are most easily triggered for you? Explain why you think this occurs.

Worksheet 3.2: Hot Buttons

Name:

All of us have hot buttons—situations we react to with strong emotion. Hot buttons develop in many ways; they can be based on past experiences or values that you've learned. Some common hot buttons are:

- Lack of fairness
- Lack of acceptance
- Criticism
- Lack of respect
- Being teased by someone (parent, teammate)
- Sensitivity about some aspect of who you are (for example, appearance, ethnicity, intelligence, lack of skill in an area)
- Negativity

List other possible hot buttons here:

1. Think about the last incident at home or school when you got really *angry*. Identify the two or three buttons that could have been "pushed." List them here.

2. Analyze what happened once the button got pushed. Did you withdraw? Over-react? Lash out? Become stressed? Describe both your *internal feelings* and your *external behaviors*.

   a. Internal feelings:

   b. External behaviors:

3. Name two specific things you could have done to manage your emotions or behavior better.

   a.

   b.

Reflection Questions

1. What will need to change for you to be able to handle the situation differently the next time your *anger* hot button gets pushed?

2. What can you do now to prepare for that?

Worksheet 3.3: ABCDE Exercise— The Impact of Thoughts on Emotions and Behaviors

Name:

Read through the following example. Then identify a recent episode (activating event) in which you engaged in irrational beliefs (B). Please keep your answers simple. Do not tell the whole story; rather, summarize with statements; for example, "My coach yelled at me" or "I made a C on an important test."

Example:

A = **A**ctivating Event: I found out my friend is going out with someone I wanted to go out with in the past.

B = (irrational) **B**elief: My friend does not care about me or my feelings.

C = **C**onsequences of the irrational belief:

Emotional: Feeling sad, angry at friend

Behavioral: Refuse to respond to friend's text

D = **D**ispute (the irrational belief): I have not talked about wanting to go out with that person in over a year. I'm dating someone else now.

E = (new) **E**ffect:

Emotional: Less sad (although I would still like to have dated that person); not angry

Behavioral: Answer friend's text

Now it's your turn! Think about a time when you may have overreacted to a situation or handled a situation poorly. Using the example as a model, fill in the blanks.

1. What was the *activating* event (A)?

2. What was your *irrational* belief or beliefs (B)?

3. What *consequences* (C) were caused by your irrational belief?
   a. Emotional consequences

   b. Behavioral consequences

4. What are some ways to *dispute* (D) your irrational belief?
   a. Provide at least two other explanations for the cause of the activating event or how you can interpret it in a more rational way than your response to #2.

   b. Provide at least one piece of disputing evidence from your past interactions with this person.

5. What would be the new *effects* (E) for you if you replaced your irrational belief with a more rational one?
   a. Emotional effects

   b. Behavioral effects

Reflection Questions

Most of our irrational beliefs fall into broad categories related to assumptions we make about . . .

1. Competence or achievement: "I must always make an A" or "I should be a starting player."
2. Relationships: "Everybody should like me" or "Others should always treat me well and look after me" or "I need to be popular."
3. Our right to happiness: "Other people should ensure my happiness, and if they don't, I have a right to be miserable" or "My needs are more important than others' needs" or "If only *x* would change, then I would be happy."

Look back at the recent episode you described earlier. Does your irrational belief relate more to competence, relationships or happiness? Explain. If you think it doesn't relate to any of these, identify an alternative reason behind your irrational belief.

Suppose some part of your irrational belief is true. For example, none of us is liked by everyone! What is a more rational statement to tell yourself when you know someone doesn't like you?

Why do people hold on to their irrational beliefs? What do they gain by doing this? What is gained by disputing your irrational beliefs?

Worksheet 3.4: Hot Buttons on Reality TV

Name:

Pick a reality TV show (such as *The Amazing Race, Survivor, The Bachelor, Top Chef*, or any other one of your choosing) or a comedy (such as *The Office, 30 Rock, or Modern Family*). Find a scene where one of the characters has a hot button pushed.

Write down the episode title, date, or number:

- Summarize the scene you watched. Include which character had a hot button pushed and what situation pushed it.

- What emotion(s) did the person display when the button was pushed?

- What behaviors did the person display when the button was pushed?

- How did other people who were around the person react?

- Was the person more or less effective in interactions **after** the hot button got pushed? Explain.

Reflection Questions

1. It's often easier to identify when others' hot buttons get pushed rather than our own. What signals can you cue into to better recognize when your hot buttons have been pushed?
2. Ask a good friend or family member how he or she knows when one of your hot buttons has been pushed. Compare that person's answer to your answer to question 1.

Worksheet 3.5: Positive and Negative Affect

Name:

Go to www.authentichappiness.com and create a user profile. All of your information will remain confidential.

On the home page, scroll through the Questionnaires Menu to find this link: PANAS Questionnaire

Log in and take the PANAS (Positive and Negative Affect Survey) questionnaire.

Reflection Questions

1. What was your level of positive and negative affect? Were you surprised by your level of positive or negative affect? Explain.
2. All of us have ups and downs and will experience positive and negative emotions. What do you consider an acceptable balance of positive and negative affect for you? Explain.

Worksheet 3.6: Self-Development Plan for Emotional Self-Awareness

Name:

Part 1. Developing a Plan for Improvement

1. Describe at least one way you will personally benefit if you increase your emotional self-awareness.

2. Choose two of the strategies listed in Appendix A for improving your emotional self-awareness and write them here. Or come up with your own strategies. Identify the dates you will begin using your strategies.

   Date to begin:

   Strategy 1:

   Date to begin:

   Strategy 2:

Part 2. Outcomes of Your Plan

Complete this part two weeks after you have implemented your strategies.

1. Describe what happened when you began using the above strategies. (If you never tried the strategies or gave up quickly, explain why you weren't motivated to give the strategies a chance to work.)
2. Do you think you will continue to use these strategies? Explain why or why not.

Self-Regard

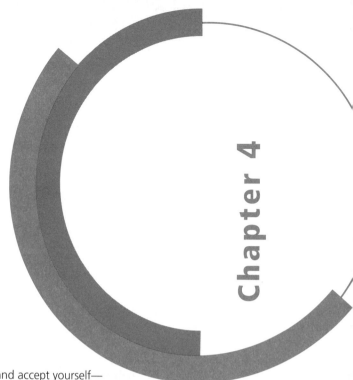

Chapter 4

Self-Regard is the ability to respect and accept yourself—
essentially liking the way you are . . . It's knowing your strengths and
weaknesses, and liking yourself, "warts and all." This conceptual component
of emotional intelligence is associated with general feelings of security, inner
strength, self-assuredness, self-confidence, and self-adequacy.
—Stein and Book, 2011, p. 68

What is self-regard? "I'm okay, you're okay"—or so people liked to say in the 1960s. Part of self-regard involves respecting yourself as you are, or believing "I'm okay." Do you understand both your strengths and your weaknesses? How much do you like and respect yourself as you are right now? Are you confident? Your answers to these questions will reflect your level of self-regard. But before we go too far, let's be clear that someone with strong self-regard will not necessarily come across as cocky. You can respect, like, and accept yourself without being conceited or brash. In fact, someone who comes across as cocky may not accept him or herself and therefore hide behind the cockiness. Or the person may like him- or herself so much there is no awareness of any weaknesses. But we all have weaknesses, and recognizing our weaknesses gives us a chance to improve. The key is to like ourselves despite our weaknesses and to keep striving for improvement while remaining self-accepting and self-confident.

Why Self-Regard?

Think about times you feel confident. We all need confidence and self-respect to perform our best. But we also need awareness of our weaknesses if we hope to prevent them from creating performance gaps, relationship problems, or a possible lack of confidence in the future. Finally, if we know our strengths, we can better leverage those strengths across a variety of situations.

Behaviors That Demonstrate Effective Self-Regard

- Being able to describe specific strengths and specific weaknesses about your current behavior or performance
- Engaging in positive self-talk (inside your head!), such as "I can do this task well because of _____ skill or knowledge"
- Being willing to take on new challenges or difficult tasks

Behaviors That Demonstrate a Need to Develop Self-Regard

- Denying that you have weaknesses because that might make you look weak to others
- Engaging in self-criticism such as "I'm so stupid" or "I can't do anything right" or "No wonder I didn't make the team"
- Not delegating a task to someone else who possesses a lot of strength in an area that may be weaker for you

Worksheet 4.1: Who Am I?

Name:

Fill in each quadrant in the table. Listing is fine. Be honest about your limitations!

My strengths are . . .	My weaknesses (areas to improve) are . . .
I feel most confident when . . .	I feel least confident when . . .

Reflection Questions

1. What surprises you the most, looking at your completed chart?
2. What connections do you see between your strengths and your areas of confidence?
3. What connections do you see between your weaknesses and your confidence?
4. How can you strengthen your areas of weakness?

Worksheet 4.2: Locus of Control Scale (Rotter, 1966)

Name:

For each item, circle either a or b. Do not skip any items.

1. a. Children get into trouble because their parents punish them too much.
   b. The trouble with most children nowadays is that their parents are too easy with them.
2. a. Many of the unhappy things in people's lives are partly due to bad luck.
   b. People's misfortunes result from the mistakes they make.
3. a. One of the major reasons why we have wars is because people don't take enough interest in politics.
   b. There will always be wars, no matter how hard people try to prevent them.
4. a. In the long run people get the respect they deserve in this world.
   b. Unfortunately, an individual's worth often passes unrecognized no matter how hard he tries.
5. a. The idea that teachers are unfair to students is nonsense.
   b. Most students don't realize the extent to which their grades are influenced by accidental happenings.
6. a. Without the right breaks one cannot be an effective leader.
   b. Capable people who fail to become leaders have not taken advantage of their opportunities.
7. a. No matter how hard you try, some people just don't like you.
   b. People who can't get others to like them don't understand how to get along with others.
8. a. Heredity plays the major role in determining one's personality.
   b. It is one's experiences in life that determine what one is like.
9. a. I have often found that what is going to happen will happen.
   b. Trusting to fate has never turned out as well for me as making a decision to take a definite course of action.
10. a. In the case of the well-prepared student, there is rarely, if ever, such a thing as an unfair test.
    b. Many times exam questions tend to be so unrelated to course work that studying is really useless.
11. a. Becoming a success is a matter of hard work; luck has little or nothing to do with it.
    b. Getting a good job depends mainly on being in the right place at the right time.
12. a. The average citizen can have an influence in government decisions.
    b. This world is run by the few people in power, and there is not much the little guy can do about it.
13. a. When I make plans, I am almost certain that I can make them work.
    b. It is not always wise to plan too far ahead because many things turn out to be a matter of good or bad fortune anyhow.

14. a. There are certain people who are just no good.
    b. There is some good in everybody.
15. a. In my case, getting what I want has little or nothing to do with luck.
    b. Many times we might just as well decide what to do by flipping a coin.
16. a. Who gets to be the boss often depends on who was lucky enough to be in the right place first.
    b. Getting people to do the right thing depends on ability; luck has little or nothing to do with it.
17. a. As far as world affairs are concerned, most of us are the victims of forces we can neither understand nor control.
    b. By taking an active part in political and social affairs, the people can control world events.
18. a. Most people don't realize the extent to which their lives are controlled by accidental happenings.
    b. There really is no such thing as "luck."
19. a. One should always be willing to admit mistakes.
    b. It is usually best to cover up one's mistakes.
20. a. It is hard to know whether or not a person really likes you.
    b. How many friends you have depends on how nice a person you are.
21. a. In the long run the bad things that happen to us are balanced by the good ones.
    b. Most misfortunes are the result of lack of ability, ignorance, laziness, or all three.
22. a. With enough effort we can wipe out political corruption.
    b. It is difficult for people to have much control over the things politicians do in office.
23. a. Sometimes I can't understand how teachers arrive at the grades they give.
    b. There is a direct connection between how hard I study and the grades I get.
24. a. A good leader expects people to decide for themselves what they should do.
    b. A good leader makes it clear to everybody what their jobs are.
25. a. Many times I feel that I have little influence over the things that happen to me.
    b. It is impossible for me to believe that chance or luck plays an important role in my life.
26. a. People are lonely because they don't try to be friendly.
    b. There's not much use in trying too hard to please people; if they like you, they like you.
27. a. There is too much emphasis on athletics in high school.
    b. Team sports are an excellent way to build character.
28. a. What happens to me is my own doing.
    b. Sometimes I feel that I don't have enough control over the direction my life is taking.
29. a. Most of the time I can't understand why politicians behave the way they do.
    b. In the long run the people are responsible for bad government on a national level, as well as on a local level.

Note: Six answers are not factored into your score: 1, 8, 14, 19, 24, and 27.

Score 1 point for each of the following:

2b	16b
3a	17b
4a	18b
5a	20b
6b	21b
7b	22a
9b	23b
10a	25b
11a	26a
12a	28a
13a	29b
15a	

My total score is _____ (0–23)

External = 11 and below with a lower score (closer to 0) reflects more externality; people with an external locus of control are more likely to believe that external circumstances—ranging from other people's behavior to fate or luck—are the primary explanation for what happens to them in life.

Internal = 13 or higher with a higher score (closer to 23) reflects more internality (note that this is reverse-scored from the original Rotter scale); people with an internal locus of control tend to explain events based on their ability, skill, or effort; in other words, they take responsibility for what happens.

Reflection Questions

1. What is your reaction to your results?
2. What do you believe are some of the benefits and consequences of having an external locus of control?
3. What do you believe are some of the benefits and consequences of having an internal locus of control?
4. What connection do you see between your self-regard and locus of control?

Worksheet 4.3: Positive and Negative Self-Talk

Name:

Positive self-talk and negative self-talk are internal messages we give ourselves, sometimes without even knowing that we do it! A good way to cue into your positive and negative self-talk is to pay attention to behaviors related to either persisting or giving up, then analyze your internal self-talk that accompanied the behavior. Fill in the following chart.

Constructive Behaviors:	Related Positive Self-Talk:
The last time I kept trying to master something hard in my academic work, a sport, or an activity was . . .	And what I said to myself to help me keep trying was . . .
The last time I did something I was scared to do was . . .	And what I said to myself to help me overcome my fear was . . .
Destructive Behaviors:	**Related Negative Self-Talk:**
The last time I gave up while trying to master academic work was . . .	And what I said to myself was . . .
The last time I did not try to do something because I lacked confidence was . . .	And what I said to myself that held me back was . . .

Reflection Questions

1. How aware were you before this assignment of your self-talk? How has your awareness level changed as you go through your day?
2. Do your negative messages follow a pattern of criticizing some aspect of yourself, such as your physical appearance, your intelligence, or your popularity? If so, explain what causes this.
3. Which of your positive messages is most helpful to you? How can you use this message more frequently?
4. What is your ratio of positive self-talk to negative self-talk? What is the consequence to you of your current ratio? (a) I use much more positive self-talk than negative self-talk; (b) I use more positive self-talk than negative self-talk; (c) I use them about the same amount; (d) I use more negative self-talk than positive self-talk; (e) I use much more negative self-talk than positive self-talk.

Worksheet 4.4: 360° Feedback

Name:

People who know you well will know your strengths and weaknesses. Ask three people who know you well to give you a list of three to five of your strengths and three to five of your weaknesses. Record them in the following chart.

Name of person giving you feedback	Strengths	Weaknesses

Reflection Questions

1. What are the common themes about your strengths? Weaknesses?
2. What strengths and weaknesses surprised you the most?
3. How did it feel to have others comment on your strengths? Your weaknesses?

Worksheet 4.5: *Modern Family*

Name:

Watch an episode of *Modern Family* (or another show assigned by your instructor) and record specific comments made by the characters or behaviors they engaged in that reflected self-awareness of strengths and/or weaknesses.

Character	Incident or Comment	Strength or Weakness?

Reflection Questions

1. Which character do you believe has the most well-developed self-regard? Explain.
2. Which character do you believe has the least well-developed self-regard? Explain.

Worksheet 4.6: Self-Development Plan for Self-Regard

Name:

Part 1. Developing a Plan

1. Describe at least one way you will personally benefit if you increase your self-regard.

2. Choose two of the strategies listed in Appendix A for improving your self-regard and write them here. Or come up with your own strategies. Identify the dates you will begin using your strategies.
    Date to begin:
    Strategy 1:

    Date to begin:
    Strategy 2:

Part 2. Outcomes of Your Plan

Complete this part two weeks after you have implemented your strategies.
1. Describe what happened when you began using your strategies. (If you never tried the strategies or tried but gave up quickly, explain why you weren't motivated to give the strategies a chance to work.)

2. Do you think you will continue to use these strategies? Explain why or why not.

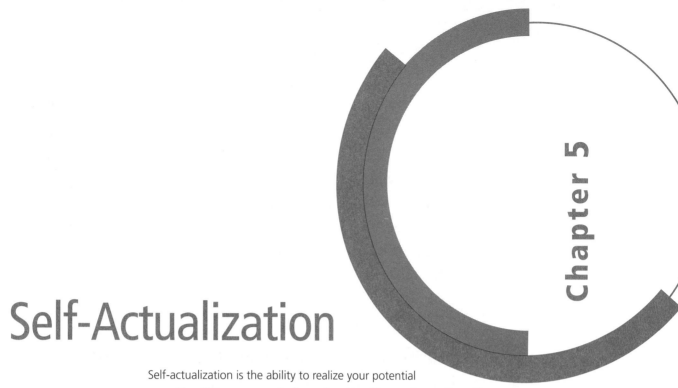

Self-Actualization

Self-actualization is the ability to realize your potential capacities. This component of emotional intelligence is manifested by your becoming involved in pursuits that lead to a meaningful, rich, and full life. Self-actualization is an ongoing, dynamic process of striving toward the maximum development of your abilities and talents, of persistently trying to do your best and to improve yourself in general.
—Stein and Book, 2011, p. 76

What is self-actualization? The term "self-actualization" sounds very lofty, doesn't it? You may imagine sitting high on a mountain peak contemplating the meaning of life. Or you may think that self-actualization means you have your life plan determined. Thankfully, it doesn't mean either one! It does mean that your actions are guided by a sense of purpose, that you have goals, and that you are receiving meaning and enjoyment from pursuing things that interest you. And it means you are striving to improve. As you grow older and move through different stages of life, your goals and purposes will change. Thus we are never finished being self-actualized!

Why Self-Actualization?

Research with college students indicates that those who have a defined purpose for being in college make better grades and are more likely to graduate in a shorter period of time (Pascarella & Terenzini, 2005). Can you imagine wanting to study hard in a major you didn't like just because you thought you'd make lots of money in that field? If you don't like the field now, why would you want to spend your life pursuing that work? Adults who possess self-actualization are often happier in both their personal and professional lives. Those seem like pretty good reasons to strive for self-actualization!

Behaviors That Demonstrate Effective Self-Actualization

- Being able to describe . . .
  - What motivates you
  - Your goals
  - What gives you enjoyment
  - What helps you feel fulfilled
  - Thinking about your next steps

Behaviors That Demonstrate a Need to Develop Self-Actualization

- Changing majors frequently (college students only)
- Trying lots of different activities but not finding one you want to stick with
- Not getting enjoyment from the things you've chosen to be involved in
- Not getting enjoyment from academic work
- Not knowing what big thing you want to do next
- Doing what your parents want, regardless of your preferences
- Avoiding courses because you don't think you could or would do well in them

Worksheet 5.1: Who Am I?

Name:

Complete the following sentence:

My favorite song title, quote, or saying is:

Now complete each quadrant of the worksheet.

My goals for my personal life are . . .	My goals for my academic work are . . .
I receive the most *enjoyment* from . . . (for example, being with friends, working on computers, science, playing basketball)	I receive the most *meaning* from . . . (for example, playing on a team, doing volunteer work)

Reflection Questions

1. Does your favorite song title express something about who you are or what goals you have? If so, explain. If not, make up a song title that describes you.
2. What experiences or people have shaped your goals?
3. Identifying goals is easier than accomplishing them. Pick your most important goal and identify what you need to do to accomplish that goal.
    a. This week?
    b. This month?
    c. This year?

Worksheet 5.2: Emotions Meter

Name:

Thinking about your goals and what gives your life meaning can create many different emotions. Circle the clip art picture(s) in Figure 5.1 that best convey(s) how you feel when thinking about your *academic, cocurricular,* and *personal* goals. Write the word *academic, cocurricular,* or *personal* for each picture you circle.

Figure 5.1 Goals Trigger Emotions

BORED   CONFUSED   STRESSED OUT

ANGRY   THOUGHTFUL   HAPPY, EXCITED

SAD   MOTIVATED

Reflection Questions

1. Pretend you are talking to your best friend. Write a brief message that summarizes what you would say to your friend about why you circled the pictures you chose.
2. Which type of goal produced your strongest emotional reaction? Explain why that goal is so important to you.
3. How do your emotional reactions affect your ability to accomplish the goal? Explain.

Worksheet 5.3: Quotes, Sayings, and Songs—A Window into You!

Name:

In the chart, write three or four meaningful sayings, quotes, song titles, song lyrics, or other words that describe or inspire you. Then write a brief description about why you chose to include each in your list.

Saying, Song Title, Lyric, or Quote	Why I like this or why it motivates me
Example: "Edge of Glory" by Lady Gaga.	This is how I felt when I almost made an A in a really difficult class; the B was good, but I knew I could have made an A if I just worked a little harder.

Reflection Question

What did you learn about yourself and your motivations by doing this exercise?

Worksheet 5.4: Defining Your Personal Mission Statement

Name:

Almost every major company, educational institution, or organization has a mission statement.

The purpose of a mission statement is to describe—in one sentence—the organization and what it hopes to accomplish or provide. For example, here are mission statements from organizations you've probably heard of:

Amazon: "Our vision is to be earth's most customer centric company; to build a place where people can come to find and discover anything they might want to buy online."
http://phx.corporate-ir.net/phoenix.zhtml?c=97664&p=irol-faq#14296
McDonald's: "Our mission is to be our customers' favorite place and way to eat."
http://www.aboutmcdonalds.com/mcd/student_zone/company_information.html
Twitter: "To instantly connect people everywhere to what's most important to them."
http://www.twitterrati.com/2011/01/11/twitters-new-mission-statement/
United States Department of State: "Create a more secure, democratic, and prosperous world for the benefit of the American people and the international community."
http://www.state.gov/s/d/rm/rls/dosstrat/2004/23503.htm

Now it's your turn. Craft a personal mission statement. Think about the questions "What do I want to do?" "For whom?" and "Why is this important?" Fulfilling your mission statement should produce enjoyment and meaning for you. Look at your answers on Worksheets 5.1 and 5.3 to help you get ideas.

My mission is . . .

Reflection Questions

1. If someone else observed your behavior for a week, would they agree that your behavior matches your mission statement? Explain your answer.
2. What are the key values reflected in your mission statement and why did you choose those?

Worksheet 5.5: *The Amazing Race*

Name:

Watch an episode of *The Amazing Race* (or another show assigned by your instructor) and record specific comments made by the characters or behaviors they engaged in that reflected self-actualization. Not all contestants are motivated just by the money. Listen and watch for other motivations!

Participant	Comment or Behavior	Self-Actualization Analysis

Reflection Questions

1. What goal statement did you find most inspiring? Explain why you chose this one.
2. If you had a chance to be on *The Amazing Race* (or other show you watched) and there was not a million-dollar prize, would you participate? Why or why not?

Worksheet 5.6: Self-Development Plan for Self-Actualization

Name:

Part 1. Developing a Plan

1. Describe at least one way you will personally benefit if you increase your self-actualization.

2. Choose two of the strategies listed in Appendix A for improving your self-actualization and write them here. Or come up with your own strategies. Identify the dates you will begin using your strategies.
   Date to begin:
   Strategy 1:

   Date to begin:
   Strategy 2:

Part 2. Outcomes of Your Plan

Complete this part two weeks after you have implemented your strategies.
1. Describe what happened when you began using the above strategies. (If you never tried the strategies or gave up quickly, explain why you weren't motivated to give the strategies a chance to work.)

2. Do you think you will continue to use these strategies? Explain why or why not.

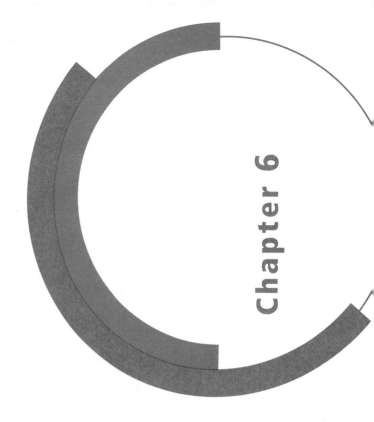

Chapter 6

Emotional Expression

Emotional expression involves openly expressing feelings both verbally and nonverbally . . . People who exhibit effective emotional expression are open and congruent in emotional messages they send to others.
—Stein and Book, 2011, p. 89

What is emotional expression? Even if you believe you don't express your emotions, you do! Nonverbal communication typically reveals more about what you're feeling than your words do. Frowning, crossing your arms, leaning back, or not looking at someone when they are talking all give cues to your emotions. And your emotions are contagious. If you smile, you are more likely to create a positive mood in others. If you frown, you can equally influence their mood in negative ways. This is called *emotional contagion*—and you've experienced it whether you realized it or not.

You learned your "rules" for emotional expression from family members. Perhaps your family yelled when angry—or withdrew silently. Perhaps expressions of anger weren't tolerated in any form, including withdrawal. Maybe you could tell family members if you were happy or excited, but if you happened to feel sad or anxious, you kept your feelings to yourself. Unfortunately, "stuffing" your emotions inside doesn't make them go away. In fact, that makes your emotions more powerful because they build up in intensity. That often results in a verbal or behavioral outburst with serious consequences.

WHY STUDY EMOTIONAL EXPRESSION?

Others will detect your inconsistencies if you give off mixed messages in your emotional expression. If you verbally indicate nothing is wrong, but nonverbally express anxiety, anger, or sadness, then others will key into the nonverbal expressions and react accordingly. Have you ever asked someone, "What's wrong?" and they say "Nothing?" But they said "nothing" using an irritated voice and with their arms folded. Chances are you didn't appreciate that mixed message. If you responded with only nonverbal expressions of your own—maybe by sighing or rolling your eyes—that just makes things worse. People can get into a vicious cycle of reacting to each other's nonverbal cues without ever talking about what is going on. So even if you think you're concealing your emotions, chances are you're not! And even if it appears that others are not reacting to your nonverbal expressions, they are! Everyone benefits from authentic verbal communication of emotions. And we all benefit from *congruence* or consistency between verbal and nonverbal emotional expression. Have the courage to express verbally what you're clearly, consistently, and frequently expressing in nonverbal ways.

Behaviors That Demonstrate Effective Emotional Expression

- Using words like "frustrated," "sad," "nervous," "happy," "excited," and "mad" as you talk with others
- Other people understand the emotion you are experiencing without having to ask you
- Using nonverbal expressions that match your words

Behaviors That Demonstrate a Need to Develop Emotional Expression

- Refusing to talk about your emotions
- Making fun of emotional expression in others
- Acting out your emotions nonverbally without talking about them
- Expressing some emotions freely (for example, anger or happiness) but squelching others (for example, sadness or fear)

Worksheet 6.1: Observing Emotions

Name:

Observe other people for one day. Watch for either verbal or nonverbal expression of the following emotions: anger, frustration, sadness, anxiety, fear, happiness, disgust, surprise. If possible, try to include some observation of children age six or younger.

Describe what the person did or said	Verbal, nonverbal, or both?	Positive or negative emotion?
Example: Student slams books down on desk (nonverbal)	Nonverbal	Negative
Example: Parent claps and yells "great play" when her child scores a goal in soccer	Nonverbal (clap); verbal ("great play")	Positive
Example: A friend seems upset and you ask what's wrong. The person frowns, crosses his arms, and says "nothing."	Nonverbal (frown, cross arms)	Negative

Worksheet 6.2: Observing Your Emotions

Name:

Observe yourself for one day. Every time you hear or see yourself express an emotion, record it in the following chart.

Describe your emotional expression	Verbal, nonverbal, or both?	Positive, negative, or both?
Example: "I'm so *excited* about our weekend plans" (said with a big smile)	Verbal, nonverbal	Positive
Example: Slamming a book down on the desk	Nonverbal	Negative

Reflection Questions

1. What types of patterns did you observe? For example, were there . . .
   - Differences in the frequency of verbal and nonverbal expressions?
   - Differences in how you expressed positive versus negative emotions?
   - Differences in how others reacted to verbal versus nonverbal expression of emotion?
   - Or in how they reacted to your expressions of positive and negative emotion?
2. What was your reaction to monitoring your emotional expression for a day?

Worksheet 6.3: Follow the Leader

Name:

Part 1

Because emotions are contagious, we can influence others to have more positive or negative emotions by our expressions of emotion. Pair up with a classmate; one of you will be the *discussion leader* and the other will be the *observer*. Then gather two or three additional friends and ask them to help you for 10 minutes with a class project. Explain that all they have to do is talk with you about their summer plans or what courses they plan to take next semester. Or pick a different topic of your choice. You should pick a topic that is neutral (strong feelings one way or the other are not likely) and a topic that would be easy for your group to discuss.

Discussion Leader. *Your job is to try to positively influence the emotion of the group.* During the 10 minutes, you should smile frequently, talk with an excited tone of voice, sit with open body language, make positive comments about your friends' comments, and use words like "happy" and "excited." Make sure your verbal and nonverbal emotions are congruent!

Observer. *Your job is to record the facial expressions and verbal emotional expressions of the other group members.* Sit where you can observe their faces and hear what they say but they cannot see what you are writing down. At one-minute intervals during the conversation, record people's facial expressions in the charts that follow. Also, record anything people say that is positive or negative; for example, "That sounds like fun" or "That sounds bad." Record both positive and negative expressions of emotion throughout the conversation.

Directions for the Conversation

1. The *discussion leader* should *open the conversation with a neutral tone* of voice and facial expression. Explain that you will have a 10-minute conversation about everyone's summer plans (or what courses they will take next semester, or a different topic of your choice). Let them know that the observer will be taking notes and that you'll let them know more about what you are doing after the discussion. (The observer should record verbal and nonverbal expressions of emotion during this time of introducing the activity.)

2. Then tell the group members you'll begin by sharing your plans. *Change your emotional expression at this point to positive!* As you tell them your plans, smile, use an excited tone of voice, and use emotion words like "excited" and "happy." Make sure you are sitting with open body language and leaning slightly forward. (The observer should be recording other people's reactions as you talk.)

3. Then ask someone else to share his or her plans. *Again, use positive emotional expression*, both verbal and nonverbal—nod in agreement, smile, sit with open body language, and say things like "That sounds like fun" (but only if that's true!). In other

words, at every opportunity when you can genuinely do so, convey positive emotions. (The observer should be scanning the group members during this time and recording their reactions.)

4. Continue the conversation in this manner for about 10 minutes or until the conversation reaches a natural end. (The observer should be recording emotional expression this whole time.)

Part 2

1. Repeat the entire activity, but this time *change your emotional expression to negative* (frustrated, angry, scared, and sad). You can use the same group of people as participated earlier or you can gather a new group of friends for the second conversation. **If you use the same group, choose a new topic**.

Directions for the Conversation

1. The *discussion leader* should *open the conversation with a neutral tone* of voice and facial expression. Explain that you will have a 10-minute conversation about everyone's summer plans (or what courses they will take next semester). Let them know that the observer will be taking notes and that you'll let them know more about what you are doing after the discussion. (The observer should record verbal and nonverbal expressions of emotion during this time of introducing the activity.)

2. Then tell the group members you'll begin by sharing your plans. *Change your emotional expression at this point to negative.* As you tell them your plans, frown, use an angry or frustrated tone of voice, and use emotion words like "frustrated," "mad," and "scared." Sit with your arms folded, lean slightly back, and frown. Use negative phrases such as "I dread . . ." (The observer should be recording other people's reactions as you talk.)

3. Then ask someone else to share his or her plans. *Again, use negative emotional expression*, both verbal and nonverbal—shake your head as if saying "No" or "That's no good," sit with closed body language, and say things like "That's no fun" or "That sounds bad" (but only if that's true!). In other words, at every opportunity when you can *genuinely* do so, convey some type of negative emotion. (The observer should be scanning the group members during this time and recording their reactions.)

4. Continue the conversation in this manner for at least 10 minutes or until the conversation reaches a natural end. (The observer should be recording emotional expression this whole time.)

5. At the end of the second discussion, tell your friends the purpose of the activity and note their reactions.

Emotional Reactions to Positive Emotions: Verbal and Nonverbal

Time	Friend #1	Friend #2	Friend #3
During directions			
At first expression of positive emotion by group leader			
1 minute later			
1 minute later			
1 minute later			
1 minute later			
1 minute later			
1 minute later			

Emotional Reactions to Negative Emotions: Verbal and Nonverbal

Time	Friend #1	Friend #2	Friend #3
During directions			
At first expression of negative emotion by group leader			
1 minute later			
1 minute later			
1 minute later			
1 minute later			
1 minute later			
1 minute later			

Reflection Questions

1. Compare and contrast the data on your two charts.
    a. How many total positive and negative expressions did you have during the positive and negative conversations?
    b. How long did it take other group members to begin responding to the leader's emotions?
    c. Which type of emotion—positive or negative—was picked up faster by other group members?
    d. What other observations can you make about your data?
2. After you told people the purpose of the conversation, what reactions did they have?

Worksheet 6.4: "I" Messages

Name:

Using "I" messages is an effective way to convey strong emotions in an appropriate way. The formula for effective "I" messages is simple:

"I feel [insert emotion word here] because [describe the behaviors of others or situation that made you feel this way] and the effect on me is [describe what impact that emotion is having on your emotions and behavior]."

For example, let's suppose you are angry at a family member because that person embarrassed you in front of friends by telling them you were grounded. An "I" message might sound like this:

"I'm mad at you because you told my friends that I was grounded and that embarrassed me so much it makes me not want to bring my friends home with me."

Here's another example: let's suppose you're frustrated because the directions for an assignment are unclear.

"I'm frustrated because I don't understand the instructions you provided for the assignment and that's made me not want to work on getting it done."

And let's take a positive emotion:

"I'm so happy because I got my acceptance letter today and all I want to do is go out and celebrate."

Part 1. Formulating "I" Messages

1. Think about a time you experienced each of the following emotions. Briefly describe the situation in the appropriate box.
2. Write down an "I" message related to each situation in its corresponding box. Write in the name of the person receiving your "I" message.

Anger

Situation:	"I" message:

Note: The recipient of the "I" message should be the person you were angry with.

Sadness

Situation:	"I" message:

Note: If a person did something to make you sad, you should direct your "I" message to that person. If a situation is making you sad (for example, a family member got diagnosed with a serious illness), your "I" message can be directed to a good friend, another family member, or someone else you trust.

Happiness or Excitement

Situation:	"I" message:

Note: If a person did something that made you happy, you should direct your "I" message to that person. If a situation is making you happy (for example, your team just won a big game), your "I" message can be directed to a good friend, another family member, or someone else you trust.

Reflection Questions

1. Would you be willing to deliver any or all of the "I" messages you wrote above to someone? Explain why or why not.
2. Which part of the "I" message formula did you have the most trouble developing? Why was that part more difficult for you?
3. Pretend someone is mad at you about something. Which of the following reactions would you want the person to choose?
   a. Give me the silent treatment for a few days and then pretend like nothing is wrong.
   b. Yell at me until all the person's anger was vented but without an opportunity for us to talk through the situation.
   c. Try to pretend like nothing is wrong, but it comes through anyway through sarcasm, facial expressions, and such.
   d. Talk to me about why he or she is mad but without yelling at me. (Note: If you choose this option, you should assume the person begins the conversation with some type of "I" message.)

   Explain why you picked your chosen option. What strategy do you use with others?

Part 2. Using Your "I" Messages

Take one of the "I" messages you developed for Part 1 of this worksheet and deliver the "I" message to the appropriate person. Deliver the message in person rather than by text, email, or phone. (Remember how important nonverbal expression of emotion is? It's much harder to understand someone else's nonverbal expression of emotion unless we are interacting face-to-face!) If you are not comfortable delivering one of the messages you developed for Worksheet 6.4, then develop a new "I" message and write it here.

Reflection Questions

1. What emotions did you feel *before* you opened a conversation using an "I" message? What about *after* you had done so?
2. Analyze how the conversation went. How was the "I" message received by the other person? What type of conversation followed? Were you satisfied with how things went?

Worksheet 6.5: TV Emotions

Name:

Watch a comedy (sitcom) on TV such as *Glee*, *Modern Family*, *30 Rock*, or *The Office*. Pick one of the main characters from the show, and as you watch, tally the times the character engages in each of the verbal or nonverbal expressions of emotion in the following charts. Fill in the blank cells with any additional behaviors observed and the number of times each occurred.

Character's Name/TV Show:

Nonverbal Expressions of Emotion

Positive Expression	Tally	Negative Expression	Tally
Smiles, laughs		Frowns	
Nods approval		Makes other type of negative facial expression	
Leans toward the other person		Rolls eyes	
Sits or stands with open body posture		Sits or stands with closed body posture (arms folded in front, hands on hips)	
Uses pleasant tone of voice (warm, appropriate volume)		Uses unpleasant tone of voice (for example, shrill, too loud, or sarcastic)	
Makes eye contact when talking to someone		Looks away when talking to someone	
Touches the person (for example, a hug or hand on shoulder)		Interrupts	

Verbal Expressions of Emotion (listen for emotion words!)

Positive Expression	Tally	Negative Expression	Tally
Happiness		Angry, irritated, upset	
Excitement		Frustrated	
Joy or love		Sad, depressed, down	
		Nervous, scared, anxious, afraid, worried	
		Disgusted	

Reflection Questions

1. Count how many tally marks you have in each of the four areas and record your results here:
   - Positive nonverbal
   - Negative nonverbal
   - Positive verbal
   - Negative verbal
2. What is your reaction to the patterns you found? How do they compare to estimates that about 90 percent of emotional expression is communicated nonverbally and 10 percent or less is communicated verbally?
3. Why do you think it's easier for most people to express emotions nonverbally than verbally?

Worksheet 6.6: Self-Development Plan for Emotional Expression

Name:

Part 1. Developing a Plan

1. Describe at least one way you will personally benefit if you increase your skill in emotional expression.

2. Choose two of the strategies listed in Appendix A for improving your emotional expression and write them here. Or come up with your own strategies. Identify the dates you will begin using your strategies.
   Date to begin:
   Strategy 1:

   Date to begin:
   Strategy 2:

Part 2. Outcomes of Your Plan

Complete this part two weeks after you have implemented your strategies.
1. Describe what happened when you began using your strategies. (If you never tried the strategies or gave up quickly, explain why you weren't motivated to give the strategies a chance to work.)

2. Do you think you will continue to use these strategies? Explain why or why not.

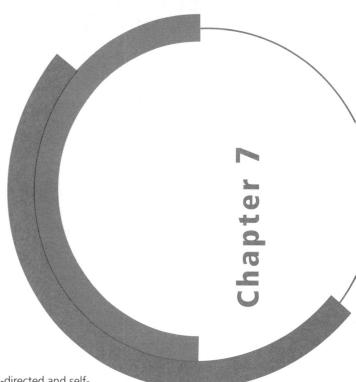

Independence

Independence is the ability to be self-directed and self-controlled in your thinking and actions and to be free of emotional dependency. Independent people are self-reliant in planning and making important decisions.
—Stein and Book, 2011, p. 96

What is independence? Independence involves being willing to act on your own, make your own decisions, and generally be free of having to rely too much on others. Independence does *not* require you to ignore others' advice or never seek different opinions. Instead, you would seek others' opinions selectively, especially when the decision has implications for that person, and for big decisions instead of everyday decisions. Independence also involves the willingness to not always follow others' advice, but you would make such a decision because of what you believe is best for you and not out of malice, defiance, or rebellion.

Research with college students indicates that students who are too independent do not fare as well in college (Mann & Kanoy, 2010). Why don't they? If you never ask for help—whether it is to complete a complicated financial aid form, seek help using a new database in the library, get tutoring when you need it, go for personal counseling, or participate in a study group—you hurt your chances for success. So the key to effective independence is having the emotional

Chapter 7

63

self-awareness and self-regard to know when it is healthy to rely on yourself and when to seek help.

WHY LEARN INDEPENDENCE?

"Why not?" might be a better question. Try to imagine how you could live life as an adult if you always needed someone else to approve of your decisions. Suppose you're in a committed romantic relationship. Would your partner want you to call your parents or best friend every time you have an argument and ask them for advice? Or suppose you have a professional job. Do you think your boss would want you to check with him or her before you made decisions that you were expected to make on your own? Being indecisive or relying on others too much puts us in an uncomfortable place. And it doesn't feel good to lack the confidence necessary to take simple actions or make simple decisions.

Behaviors That Demonstrate Effective Independence

- Going somewhere by yourself without needing someone to go with you
- Completing a difficult assignment without asking for someone to make sure you are doing it correctly
- Making an important decision after collecting the information needed
- Traveling alone (for example, by airplane cross-country or overseas)
- Earning money to pay for your social activities, cell phone, or car

Behaviors That Demonstrate a Need to Develop Independence

- Seeking approval from others for decisions, even small ones, such as what pair of shoes to buy or whether to go out with friends
- Asking others' opinions over and over before you make a decision
- Frequently checking in with faculty members about whether you are doing an assignment correctly
- Being unwilling to go somewhere alone
- Relying on others to give you money when you can earn it yourself
- Calling, texting, or otherwise wanting to be in touch with someone 24/7
- Borrowing money frequently; expecting others to pay for things most people your age pay for by themselves

Worksheet 7.1: Private Eye

Name:

Pretend you are a private investigator and your job is to observe yourself. During one 24-hour period, write down all of the times you acted independently or dependently. Listed here are four main areas of independence and examples of independent behavior:

- *Academic.* Examples: completing projects without asking the professor for help, studying alone instead of with a tutor or study group, making class choice decisions without consulting your advisor. (Note: Students who are too independent do not perform as well in college as those who have more moderate amounts of independence. They don't seek help even when they clearly need it!)
- *Financial.* Examples: earning your spending money, not asking others to bail you out if you overspend or bounce a check, opening and managing your own bank account, understanding how your credit card works.
- *Physical.* Examples: driving on a long trip by yourself, spending weeks or months away from home without getting homesick, being comfortable staying by yourself.
- *Social/emotional.* Examples: making important decisions without needing approval or reassurance from others; handling challenging situations with teachers, coaches, or bosses without others doing it for you; standing up to group pressure when you disagree with members' behaviors.

Fill in the following chart. Make sure you include at least one of each area of independence, even if you have to observe yourself for more than one day.

Situation	Type of independence	Independence or dependence?
Picked a major without getting family approval	Social/emotional	Independence
Asked parents for additional money to cover overdrawn bank account	Financial	Dependence
Found directions and drove alone to get my driver's license renewed	Physical	Independence
Went to see teacher four times for additional help on the same assignment	Academic	Dependence

Reflection Questions

1. What types of patterns do you see in terms of how much you consult others for various types of decisions?
2. Whose opinion or support is important to you, and does that vary by the type of decision?
3. What is your overall comfort level with acting independently?
4. What was your level of independence during this observation period? How much did observing your own behavior change how often you sought others' opinions or approval?
5. How did your emotional reactions to various situations relate to your level of independence?

Worksheet 7.2: By Yourself

Name:

Do something by yourself that you would normally do with others and that will make you somewhat uncomfortable to do by yourself. Go eat in a restaurant, go shopping, or go to a movie. Go talk to a faculty member about a class if that's not something you would normally do. Do *not* tell others ahead of time why you are doing this alone. *Do not pick an unsafe activity, just one you normally would not do alone.* Then answer the reflection questions below.

Reflection Questions

1. What did you do by yourself that you would normally do with others?
2. What emotions did you experience as you were deciding what to do and right before the activity? Why do you think you experienced those emotions?
3. How did you feel after you completed the activity? Explain why you felt this way.
4. (Optional) Tell someone who knows you well what you did by yourself, but do *not* tell that person why you did the activity alone. What was the person's reaction?

Worksheet 7.3: Please Do This for Me!

Name:

Go to the following link found on YouTube, for a video called "Helicopter Parents: The lengths parents go to pamper and please their kids," http://www.youtube.com/watch?v=ufEfeDP7vBA& feature=related

Part 1

Watch the YouTube clip about Anthony. Record at least three of his actions that show dependence on his mother. Then write down the consequences of those actions for Anthony. (Note: The possible long-term consequences are not evident in the YouTube clip, so use your imagination!)

Anthony's Actions	Short-Term Results	Possible Long-Term Consequences for Anthony
1.		
2.		
3.		

Part 2

Think about behaviors you've engaged in over the past year that may have been too dependent. Maybe you asked your family members to talk with a teacher or coach for you, or fill out a form for you, or give you extra money, or take care of your car for you instead of taking care of it yourself. The action could have involved friends, such as choosing what universities to apply to based on where your friends applied or not going on a school-sponsored trip unless a friend went with you. Choose the most significant incident and answer the following reflection questions.

Reflection Questions

Describe the situation in which you acted with dependence. Then answer these questions.

1. What did you do to promote your dependence on someone else?
2. How did this benefit you in the short term?
3. How might this benefit you (or not benefit you) in the long term? Explain your answer.

Worksheet 7.4: Reality TV—Too Needy, Too Alone, or Just Right?

Name:

1. Watch an episode of reality TV in which people are forced to work in groups or where one person has a lot of power and control over other people. Good shows to watch include *Survivor, The Celebrity Apprentice, The Amazing Race, Scare Tactics,* or *The Bachelor.* Feel free to watch a different show as long as three or more people have to interact in some way.

2. Pick three characters (or three different scenarios within the episode): one time when a person was too dependent on others, one time when a person was too independent, and one time when a person exhibited appropriate independence. Summarize what each of the characters did that caused you to reach the conclusion you did.

   Person/Situation A (too dependent):

   Person/Situation B (too independent):

   Person/Situation C (appropriately independent):

3. What was the outcome for each person?

4. If you had been in this situation, which character would you most resemble? Explain your answer.

Worksheet 7.5: On My Own

Name:

- Fill in the following chart based on what you think would be an appropriate age for a parent to consider letting the child engage in the activity by himself or herself. Assume the child, teen, or young adult has the skill needed to do the activity or *should* have the skill by this age.
- In the space for Other #1, list something you felt capable of doing at an earlier age than you were actually allowed to do it.
- In the space for Other #2, list something you did not feel capable of doing but were forced to do at an earlier age than you would have liked.

Activity	Appropriate age	Brief explanation for the age you chose
Pay for your cell phone		
Make your own doctor's appointment		
Open and manage your own checking account		
Talk with a teacher about a bad grade you made and what you need to do differently		
Drive on an interstate highway (assuming you got your driver's license at age 16)		
Stay home alone for one hour for the first time		

Spend the night alone in your house over the weekend while your parents travel		
Choose what courses to take the next semester		
Get your car inspected		
Make your own dinner		
Do your own laundry		
Walk five minutes to a friend's house on a sidewalk in the neighborhood (assuming the neighborhood is safe)		
Other #1		
Other #2		

Reflection Questions

1. Compare the ages you listed to the decisions your family made about you. What trends do you notice?
2. Compare your answers to what a friend or classmate answered. What conclusions can you draw from the similarities and differences between your answers?
3. Consider your response for Other #1. What was your reaction to being told you could not do this yet? In retrospect, do you agree or disagree with the decision?
4. Consider your response for Other #2. What was your reaction and how did things turn out? In retrospect, do you agree or disagree with the decision?

Worksheet 7.6: Self-Development Plan for Independence

Name:

Part 1. Developing a Plan

1. Describe at least one way you will personally benefit if you increase your independence.

2. Choose two of the strategies listed in Appendix A for improving your independence and write them here. Or come up with your own strategies. Identify the dates you will begin using your strategies.
   Date to begin:
   Strategy 1:

   Date to begin:
   Strategy 2:

Part 2. Outcomes of Your Plan

Complete this part two weeks after you have implemented your strategies.
1. Describe what happened when you began using these strategies. (If you never tried the strategies or gave up quickly, explain why you weren't motivated to give the strategies a chance to work.)

2. Do you think you will continue to use these strategies? Explain why or why not.

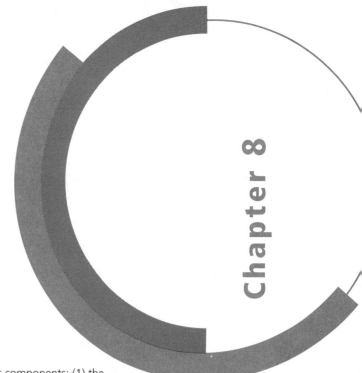

Chapter 8

Assertiveness

Assertiveness comprises three basic components: (1) the
ability to express feelings . . . (2) the ability to express beliefs and thoughts
openly . . . and (3) the ability to stand up for personal rights (not allowing others to
bother you or take advantage of you).
—Stein and Book, 2011, p. 105

What is assertiveness? Many people confuse assertiveness with aggressiveness and think that the more assertive you become, the more likely it is that you'll act aggressively. That's not accurate. Aggression always involves the intent to *harm* someone either with words or actions; in contrast, assertiveness represents standing up for yourself, your beliefs, or your feelings in a way that is *not* harmful to others. Thus assertiveness is about taking care of yourself and allowing others to know your opinions, thoughts, and feelings.

Passivity is the opposite of assertiveness. When you act passively, you allow others to take control of you or to unduly influence your thoughts, emotions, or behaviors. If you are passive, others will sometimes take advantage of you—by, for example, asking you to do far more than your fair share of the work on a project or at home. Or they may ask you to work overtime for no extra pay, and you agree.

You might believe that it's okay to be assertive with peers, but not with teachers, parents, or bosses. Because assertiveness represents healthy emotional functioning and is important to your overall well-being, you need to be assertive no matter who you are interacting with! If you are assertive and not aggressive, others almost always respond positively.

WHY ASSERTIVENESS?

Assertiveness helps you take care of yourself. Imagine yourself out with peers when someone in the group suggests doing something that is illegal or could be physically harmful to others (think of hazing). You need assertiveness in that situation in order to convince everyone that the action is wrong and if that fails, you need assertiveness to remove yourself from the group. The hazing that goes on in some fraternities and other organizations (clubs, band) and that has occasionally reached dangerous levels—costing some young people their lives—could have been stopped if one or two of the members had been assertive enough to express their concerns about the severity of the hazing. Or imagine yourself 20 years from now in a career, and your boss orders you to do something that is unethical or even illegal. Will you have the ability to assertively say "No," or will you go along? Or imagine yourself in a dating relationship right now, in which the other person continually embarrasses you in front of others by teasing you about a sensitive subject. Can you stand up for yourself? In each of these cases, assertiveness is required. Those who lack assertiveness are destined to be taken advantage of by others, to feel unimportant or frustrated, and to not get what they want because they are scared to make their needs known.

Behaviors That Demonstrate Effective Assertiveness

- Expressing your opinions in class
- Asking a boss for time off during a busy weekend to attend a big event at school
- Being able to say "No" to endless requests for your time
- Telling someone you love about something they are doing that hurts or upsets you
- Standing up to a group of people even if you don't have someone to support you

Behaviors That Demonstrate a Need to Develop Assertiveness

- Doing others' work for them when they ask you
- Never being the one to choose the restaurant, the TV show, the movie, or where to spend the evening
- Letting others take advantage of you by borrowing your car too frequently, wearing your clothing without asking, or borrowing money without paying it back because they know you won't ask for it
- Not joining in class discussions even when you have strong feelings or beliefs
- Saying "Yes" too often and overcommitting yourself, leaving too little time to do the things you want or enjoy

Worksheet 8.1: Assertive, Aggressive, or Passive?

Name:

Identify which of the behaviors in the chart are assertive, passive, or aggressive, based on the definitions given earlier in this chapter. If a behavior is either passive or aggressive, describe what an assertive response or behavior would look like in that situation.

Behavior or Incident	Assertive, Passive, or Aggressive?	Assertive Solution
You share a bathroom at home with your sister. You see her headed that way, so you race by her and lock the bathroom door behind you. She screams "Jerk!" at you through the door. Your sister's behavior was . . .		
In the scenario above, your behavior of racing by her was . . .		
Your boss asks you to work overtime during a busy weekend. You respond by saying, "Well, I was sort of hoping to go to the beach." Your response to your boss was . . .		
The editor of the student newspaper asks you to write an editorial about changes in the parking policy. You are very busy but believe students are being treated unfairly, so you agree. You agree to write the article and express your opinions about the parking situation. Writing the article was . . .		

Your dating partner asks what movie you want to see. You say, "I don't care," so your partner picks a horror movie. You hate horror movies, so you say, "Can we do something other than going to the movies?" Your response was . . .		
A faculty member assigns a long paper for students to complete over the weekend that had not been previously announced. You have a family wedding to attend. As you are leaving class, you mutter to your friend who's also in the class, "I hate this class." Your response to the paper assignment was . . .		
A partner in a dating relationship breaks up with you because things are "too intense" between you. A week later, your partner asks you to go to a movie without saying anything else. You agree without asking about the purpose of getting together. Your behavior was . . .		

Reflection Questions

1. How difficult was it for you to come up with appropriately assertive responses?
2. How likely would you be to use those assertive responses if you were faced with similar situations? Explain your answer.

Worksheet 8.2: It Seems So Easy When Others Do It

Name:

- Go to http://www.youtube.com/watch?v=Ymm86c6DAF4 and watch the 10-minute clip, "Assertiveness Scenarios: 10 Examples." There are 10 short scenarios, as listed in the following chart.

For each scenario, fill in the chart. In the Assertive, Aggressive, or Passive? column, list both characters and their reactions. If you think their reaction changed during the scenario (for example, passive but then becoming assertive) note this. In column #3, describe the long-term consequences for each character if his or her behavior continues in this way.

Scenario	Assertive, Aggressive, or Passive?	Long-Term Consequences for Each Character
#1 Asking for help		
#2 Breaking into line		
#3 Breaking into line (take 2)		
#4 McDonald's or Subway		
#5 McDonald's or Subway (take 2)		
#6 Missing tickets		
#7 Breaking up		
#8 Cover for me		
#9 Movie choice		
#10 Movie choice (take 2)		

Reflection Questions

1. Being appropriately assertive sometimes resulted in the other person's becoming aggressive. How does the potential for such a reaction influence your willingness to be assertive? Explain.

2. Which character reminds you the most of yourself? Now look at the long-term consequences you wrote down for that person. What is your reaction to those consequences?

Worksheet 8.3: Giving Feedback

Name:

Giving feedback to others requires assertiveness because in giving feedback you are stating an opinion or belief. Sometimes we avoid giving feedback either because we are concerned the other person might get angry or because we don't want to hurt someone's feelings. However, withholding honest feedback prevents us from improving relationships or helping others improve their performance.

Part 1

Refer back to Chapter 6 on emotional expression and how to deliver an "I" message. Then write down "I" messages for each of the following four scenarios:

- Give feedback to a family member about something he or she has done that hurt your feelings or upset you:

- Give feedback to a friend or dating partner about a behavior he or she engages in that annoys or upsets you:

- Give feedback to a faculty member about a way to improve a class:

- Give feedback to the head of your school about something that could be done to improve the school:

Part 2

Pick one of your responses and deliver the message to the individual *in person* (or at the least via a phone call). Do *not* use text, Facebook, messaging/chat, or email!

Reflection Questions

1. Were you able to successfully deliver the feedback in an assertive way? If so, how did the interaction turn out? If you became too passive or too aggressive, what do you think caused that?
2. What was the outcome of your delivering the feedback?
3. How did you feel before, during, and after the interaction?

Worksheet 8.4: Controversial Issues

Name:

Think about a friend or family member that you differ with on some important value such as a religious or political belief. Casually bring up the topic with the person; do not let him or her know you are doing this for a class assignment. Your goal is to stay assertive without becoming passive or aggressive.

Fill in the spaces:

- The person (and their relationship to you):

- The issue:

Remaining assertive during a challenging conversation can be difficult. Answer the following questions to help you become more aware of signals that indicate you have become passive or aggressive.

- What signs can I cue into that I am becoming too aggressive? Too passive?

- What sentence can I begin the conversation with that summarizes my belief in an assertive way?

Reflection Questions

1. Analyze how well you remained assertive throughout the conversation. If you became aggressive or passive, what triggered this behavior?
2. What cultural, religious, or family values affect your level of assertiveness, aggressiveness, or passiveness?

Worksheet 8.5: Assertiveness Quiz

Name:

Assertiveness depends on two factors: (1) our level of (dis)comfort being assertive in that situation and (2) the situation and who is involved. Rank the situations in the following chart, circling a number score based on how you would feel and behave.

Level of comfort with being assertive

1   Very uncomfortable

2   Uncomfortable

3   Comfortable

4   Very comfortable

Level of assertiveness in that situation

1   Not at all assertive (I do not stand up for myself or state my beliefs at all; passive).

2   Somewhat assertive (I make an initial attempt to be assertive but back off if the other person challenges me).

3   Assertive (I state what I want but ultimately give in or fail to fully defend my beliefs if I am repeatedly challenged).

4   Very assertive (I continue to defend my beliefs or stand up for myself without being aggressive, no matter what the other person says or does).

0   I am likely to become aggressive (I may interrupt a lot, yell, insult the other person, throw something, or storm out).

Comfort		Assertiveness
1 2 3 4	Tell a friend that he or she has done something that bothers me.	0 1 2 3 4
1 2 3 4	Ask a teacher why he or she took off points for an answer on a test.	0 1 2 3 4
1 2 3 4	Speak up in a class during a heated discussion.	0 1 2 3 4
1 2 3 4	Speak up in a group of friends when you believe someone is doing something wrong.	0 1 2 3 4
1 2 3 4	Question a rule that your family members have set for you.	0 1 2 3 4
1 2 3 4	Tell a dating partner about something that he or she has done to upset you.	0 1 2 3 4
1 2 3 4	Express your opinion about a controversial topic with friends.	0 1 2 3 4
1 2 3 4	Express your opinion about a controversial topic with family.	0 1 2 3 4
1 2 3 4	Turn down a request to help someone when you don't want to help.	0 1 2 3 4
1 2 3 4	Ask a stranger who is talking loudly during a movie to be quiet.	0 1 2 3 4

Total your comfort scores and your assertiveness. Notice that aggressiveness gets 0 points!

Reflection Questions

1. What patterns do you notice in your comfort level? In your assertiveness level?
2. Look at the items where you circled 0 for aggression. What situations are likely to promote aggression in you?
3. When you are not assertive, what do you believe is the major reason? Circle the letters for all relevant explanations.
   a. Concerned about making others angry
   b. Concerned about making things worse for myself
   c. Just don't have the energy to deal with it
   d. Don't want to risk upsetting others I care about
   e. Don't think it will change anything even if I am assertive
   f. Don't know how (don't have the skills) to be assertive
   g. Something else (explain)
4. Look at the items you circled in the previous question. What can you learn about yourself from reviewing this list?

Worksheet 8.6: Self-Development Plan for Assertiveness

Name:

Part 1. Developing a Plan

1. Describe at least one way you will personally benefit if you increase your skill in developing assertiveness.

2. Choose two of the strategies listed in Appendix A for improving your assertiveness and write them below. Or come up with your own strategies. Identify the dates you will begin using your strategies.
   Date to begin:
   Strategy 1:

   Date to begin:
   Strategy 2:

Part 2. Outcomes of Your Plan

Complete this part two weeks after you have implemented your strategies.

1. Describe what happened when you began using your strategies. (If you never tried the strategies or gave up quickly, explain why you weren't motivated to give the strategies a chance to work.)

2. Do you think you will continue to use these strategies? Explain why or why not.

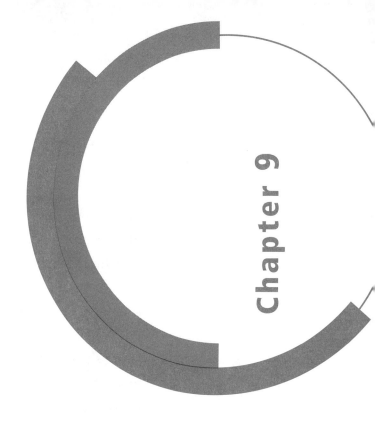

Chapter 9

Interpersonal Relationship

By interpersonal relationships, we mean the ability to establish and maintain mutually satisfying relationships that are characterized by the ability to both "give" and "take" in relationships, and where trust and compassion are openly expressed in words or by behavior.
—Stein and Book, 2011, p. 125

What is interpersonal relationship? Think about the last time you interacted with someone who was comfortable letting you get to know him or her beyond the basic facts like his or her favorite activities, academic interests, and favorite music. People who are skilled at interpersonal relations are good at getting to know others and letting others get to know them. Instead of being scared by the possibility of a meaningful connection, they welcome it. Additionally, people good at interpersonal relationships trust others and thus are comfortable being vulnerable and expect positive results from such interactions.

WHY INTERPERSONAL RELATIONSHIP?

Life is richer when we share it in meaningful ways with others. Although you may worry about getting hurt, a life spent without meaningful relationships with others is also devoid of great moments of joy and connection. Almost every study that talks about coping well with stress includes "social support" as a form of positive coping. It's difficult to have social support if you don't have others that you are meaningfully connected with! Living in the same space or sharing common goals does not guarantee that you have a meaningful relationship with someone. Getting to know that person beyond a surface level, sharing hopes and fears, and letting that person get to know the real you is what guarantees a meaningful relationship. So far, you may think this sounds just fine for your social or personal life but not important in your work life. Actually, strong interpersonal relationship skills—while likely to be less intense and less personal in a work situation—predict greater success in a variety of careers. Think about it—who would you rather work for, a boss who knows something about you and what's important to you or one that knows only your name and your productivity level?

Behaviors That Demonstrate Effective Interpersonal Relationship

- Being able to name the most important person in your life and explain why
- Trying to get to know friends by asking questions that go beyond surface details
- Going beyond surface details when a friend asks you about yourself
- Rarely thinking in terms of "getting hurt" by others; rather, thinking in terms of "getting to know" others
- Rarely or never being too busy to sit down and have a conversation with someone
- Those you call your "best friends" knowing personal information about you

Behaviors That Demonstrate a Need to Develop Interpersonal Relationships

- Giving vague answers like "sometimes," "okay," or "I'm not sure" when asked a question about yourself
- On a group project, focusing only on the task and not getting to know the people you are working with
- Getting nervous or uncomfortable if someone asks you a personal question
- Rarely or never asking others to give you meaningful information about them
- Keeping your conversations at a surface level—the upcoming game, what assignment you're working on, or what classes you're taking
- Finding it hard to trust others

Worksheet 9.1: My Favorite Person

Name:

Part 1

Other than one of your parents or guardians, think about the person with whom you have the most meaningful relationship. Answer the following questions about that person. If you're not sure of the answer to a question, skip it for now.

What (who) is this person's . . .

- Favorite color:

- Favorite book or type of book:

- Favorite sport:

- Best friend (other than you!):

- Favorite thing to do in his or her free time:

- Greatest source of joy:

- Greatest source of sadness or anxiety:

- Biggest accomplishment in life:

- Biggest disappointment in life:

Part 2

Now contact the person and go over the answers to make sure you were correct (or close) in what you said. If you didn't know what to write down, ask the person that question.

Reflection Questions

1. What makes this person special to you?
2. How likely is it that the person knows the same amount of information about you as you did about him or her?
3. What is your reaction to what you knew about this "special" person? Was the amount you knew just right, too much, or too little, given how you feel about this person? Explain your answer.

Worksheet 9.2: Sharing Secrets

Name:

Go to http://www.youtube.com/watch?v=2XkLOT9J1vs&feature=fvst and watch the YouTube clip called "Sharing Secrets—Saints and Soldiers." If this clip is not active, the movie *Saints and Soldiers* is also available on hulu.com; the assigned scene is about 31 minutes into the movie. If these sources are no longer available, use the scene from the movie *Notting Hill* in which all of the adults are sitting around the dinner table and decide to share something very personal (about 25–30 minutes into the movie). Next, answer the reflection questions. Your class leader should make it clear ahead of time whether you will have to turn in your responses to these questions.

Reflection Questions

1. What secret would you have told in that group? Or would you have refused to tell one?
2. As you were watching the clip, how did your feelings or thoughts about each person change? For example, were you turned off by the sharing, did it make you like the person more, or what other reaction did you have?
3. If you had been the soldier who asked the last guy what his secret was, how would you have responded (internally and externally) to his response?
4. What is your biggest concern about sharing a secret?
5. What is the best thing that's ever happened to you because you did share a secret?

Worksheet 9.3: Scaling the Intimacy Wall

Name:

Consider each area of the following table. Fill in what types of personal details (such as your joys, troubles, dreams, disappointments, interests, and activities) you would be comfortable telling someone based on the relevant quadrant. You can either fill in a word like "disappointments" or briefly describe your actual disappointments. Your class leader should tell you ahead of time whether this worksheet will be turned in or shared with anyone else.

	Know Person Well	**Person Is an Acquaintance**
Desire Close Relationship	What I would share about myself is . . .	What I would share about myself is . . .
Desire Less Close Relationship (But Not Distant)	What I would share about myself is . . .	What I would share about myself is . . .

Reflection Questions

1. Which quadrant did you have the most difficulty completing? Explain why that one was the most difficult.
2. In real life, which of the types of interpersonal relationships listed in the table do you struggle with the most in terms of revealing enough but not too much about yourself? Explain.

The Student EQ Edge: Student Workbook

Worksheet 9.4: Beginning a Relationship

Name:

1. Pick out someone you barely know from your school, a team you're on, a group you belong to, or some other area of your life. The next time you see that person, approach him or her and begin a conversation. Who do you plan to approach? If you don't know his or her name, describe the person.

2. Write down at least three good opening comments that would help you get a conversation started. The first one may not work, but chances are one of the other two will.

3. Once you have had the conversation, write a brief summary of what you talked about. Then answer the following questions:
    *   How long did you talk?

    *   Did the other person talk about the same amount as you did, or more or less?

    *   Did you get to know the person better?

    *   Do you plan on having another conversation or doing something with that person?

Reflection Questions

1. Explain whether this experience will make you more willing to have this type of conversation in the future.
2. What were your biggest concerns or fears before the conversation?
3. How did you feel after the conversation?

Worksheet 9.5: Getting Closer

Name:

This worksheet is similar to Worksheet 9.4, except that now you are going to repeat the activity with someone you know fairly well but would like to get to know better. Think about "scaling the intimacy wall" and trying to let the other person learn something new about you.

1. Who do you plan to approach? What topic do you want to talk about?

2. Write down at least three good opening comments that would help you get a conversation started.

3. Once you have had the conversation, write a brief summary of what you talked about. Then answer the following questions:
   * Did you get to know the person better?

   * Do you feel closer to the person as a result of the conversation?

   * Do you plan on having another conversation or doing something with that person?

Reflection Questions

1. Explain whether this experience will make you more willing to have this type of conversation in the future.
2. What were your biggest concerns or fears before the conversation?
3. How did you feel after the conversation?
4. If you have completed Worksheet 9.4, compare and contrast the conversation you had with someone you did not know well and the one you had with someone you already know well but would like to get to know better. Which type of conversation is easier for you? What does that tell you about yourself?

Worksheet 9.6: Self-Development Plan for Interpersonal Relationship

Name:

Part 1. Developing a Plan

1. Describe at least one way you will personally benefit if you increase your skill in developing interpersonal relationships.

2. Choose two of the strategies listed in Appendix A for improving your interpersonal relationships and write them here. Or come up with your own strategies. Identify the dates you will begin using your strategies.
    Date to begin:
    Strategy 1:

    Date to begin:
    Strategy 2:

Part 2. Outcomes of Your Plan

Complete this part two weeks after you have implemented your strategies.
1. Describe what happened when you began using these strategies. (If you never tried the strategies or gave up quickly, explain why you weren't motivated to give the strategies a chance to work.)

2. Do you think you will continue to use these strategies? Explain why or why not.

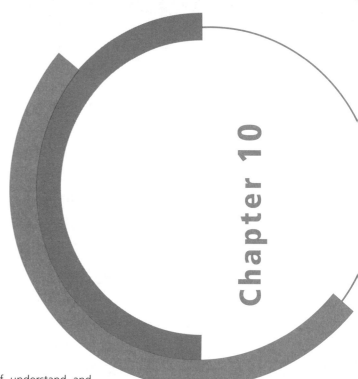

Chapter 10

Empathy

Empathy is the ability to be aware of, understand, and
appreciate the feelings and thoughts of others. Empathy is "tuning in" (being
sensitive) to what, how, and why people feel and think the way they do.
—Stein and Book, 2011, p. 134

What is empathy? Alfred Adler eloquently described
empathy as seeing, hearing, or feeling as if you were someone else. But before we can see, hear, or feel as another person
might, we must first be *aware of the need to do that*! Before we can
be empathic, we have to care about other people or the situation
enough to be concerned about or interested in their views. How
many times have you been in a heated discussion with someone
else and, while that person was talking, you were thinking about
what you wanted to say next? We've all done it. Sometimes we
want to "win" so much that we're willing to sacrifice the long-term
health of a relationship or the other person's feelings in order to
make sure our points are understood. Being empathic, though,
does *not* mean that you have to agree with others' opinions or
give in to what they want. Rather, it means that you try hard to
understand their perspective both cognitively (the reason for
their views) and emotionally (the emotions they are feeling).

● WHY EMPATHY?

As you read the preceding description, you may have wondered what you have to gain by being empathic. Here are three good reasons to be empathic. First, when you try hard to understand someone else's perspective, you can experience a genuine change of perspective yourself. In other words, listening gives you a chance to learn new information, which may change your opinion. Second, when you try to understand others, you will often help defuse a tense situation. All of us want to know that others care about our thoughts and feelings and we tend to calm down when we believe someone else is listening. Third, you will have much healthier, happier relationships at home, school, and work if you develop empathy because you will have a richer understanding of the people you interact with the most.

Behaviors That Demonstrate Effective Empathy

- Listening to others without interrupting
- Being able to accurately summarize what others have said
- Being able to accurately determine what the other person is feeling
- Asking questions to help you understand others' points of view
- Imagining how things look or feel to the other people involved in a situation

Behaviors That Demonstrate a Need to Develop Empathy

- Interrupting while others are talking
- Thinking about what points you want to make instead of listening to someone else
- Believing your perspective is always more correct or better than other people's
- Not caring whether you hurt someone else's feelings
- Not being able to imagine something from another's perspective (or not even realizing why this is important!)
- Being unable to emotionally connect to someone else who is having an intense emotion
- Making fun of people who are different from you

Worksheet 10.1: What Is Empathy?

Name:

Imagine that you are really upset about something and begin telling a friend about it. In the space after each possible response from your friend, note whether this would *help* or *not help* you and give a brief reason why.

	Helpful?	Why or why not?
1. "I had the same thing happen to me once" (the friend then begins to tell you the story, which takes several minutes).		
2. "That sounds pretty bad. No wonder you're mad."		
3. "What else happened?"		
4. "There's no need to get so upset. You won't be able to decide what you want to do."		
5. "It sounds like . . ." (the friend then summarizes how he or she thinks you feel and why, such as "It sounds like you're pretty ticked off because Chris made fun of you in front of so many people").		
6. "Don't worry about it. If you act like you don't care, the other person won't know they upset you."		
7. "Wow, I can see why you're so upset."		

Reflection Questions

1. Which two of these responses would make you most likely to keep talking about the issue?
2. Which two responses would make you least likely to keep talking?
3. Which of the responses do you most often use? Explain why you use this one.

Worksheet 10.2: The Art of Questions

Name:

Open-ended questions keep other people talking, giving you a better chance to understand their thoughts, feelings, or opinions. These questions avoid judgment, do not lead the other person to a particular response, and cannot be answered with just one word. Pretend that someone has just made each of the following comments to you. Write an open-ended question you could ask to learn more about that person's perspective.

Example: "That math test was unfair."
Question: "Which questions or problems made you think it was unfair?"

1. "I can't stand it when she nags me so much."
   Question:

2. "He was a real jerk."
   Question:

3. "You made me mad when you didn't answer my text."
   Question:

4. "I don't think capital punishment is right under any circumstance."
   Question:

5. "I think your opinion about abortion is wrong."
   Question:

6. "I'm so excited."
   Question:

Reflection Questions

1. Which types of questions or comments were the hardest for you to respond to? Why do you think that is so?
2. How likely are you to use any of these responses in a real conversation? Explain your answer.

Worksheet 10.3: Reflective Listening

Name:

Reflective listening means you are able to accurately summarize the content and meaning of someone's thoughts or ideas, including any feelings that may have been expressed explicitly or implicitly. Don't just repeat what the person says (that tends to sound silly); instead, rephrase it so the person knows you really listened.

Example: "The coach didn't even give me a fair chance. I made one mistake and got pulled out of the game and never went back in. How's that fair when Kelly got to stay in after allowing that goal? I think the coach doesn't like me for some reason. I wonder if it's even worth it to play."

Reflective Listening Response: "You sound pretty frustrated with soccer, and you're steamed at the coach."

Now, write reflective listening responses to each of the following statements:

"I can't stand this class. The teacher demands so much work, he must think it's the only class we have. The material is so boring that I fall asleep every time I try to read the book."
Reflective listening response:

"I never have enough money. I never get to go out with friends and always have to work as many hours as I can. I'm sick of it."
Reflective listening response:

"I can't believe you teased me about my clothes in front of all those people. What were you thinking?"
Reflective listening response:

Reflection Questions

1. Read back over the scenarios. What do you think is the person's primary emotion in each scenario?
   a. Scenario #1
   b. Scenario #2
   c. Scenario #3
2. How do you typically react when you hear someone express those emotions?
3. What will be the hardest thing for you about doing reflective listening in real situations?

Worksheet 10.4: Empathy Assessment

Name:

Respond to the following statements using the number scale.

1 = Strongly disagree **2 = Disagree** **3 = Slightly disagree** **4 = Slightly agree** **5 = Agree** **6 = Strongly agree**

1. Seeing someone who is upset makes me upset.

   1   2   3   4   5   6

2. I tend to cry during sad movies.

   1   2   3   4   5   6

3. I think it's funny when others get teased and get upset about it.

   1   2   3   4   5   6

4. I get upset when someone is mistreated.

   1   2   3   4   5   6

5. When I see a homeless person on the side of the road asking for money, I get mad at the person for begging.

   1   2   3   4   5   6

6. I like hearing about friends doing well in school even if I'm not doing as well as I want to.

   1   2   3   4   5   6

7. When someone gets mad at me, I try to understand why that person is mad.

   1   2   3   4   5   6

8. When a friend complains about something I think is trivial, I stop listening.

   1   2   3   4   5   6

9. I have a hard time listening to someone else's opinion without arguing when the person's opinion differs from mine.

| 1 | 2 | 3 | 4 | 5 | 6 |

10. I can tell you the other person's main concerns even during the heat of an argument.

| 1 | 2 | 3 | 4 | 5 | 6 |

Scoring: For items 3, 5, 8, and 9, change your scores as follows: if you circled a 1, change it to 6; change a 2 to a 5, a 3 to a 4, a 4 to a 3, a 5 to a 2, and a 6 to a 1. Then add up your points for your first five items—this is your emotional empathy. Then add the scores for items 6–10. This is your cognitive empathy. The higher your score (maximum total = 30 for each section), the more empathic you think you are.

Now give these same 10 questions to the person you believe knows you the best and ask him or her to think about you when responding. (Do *not* tell the person your scores first.) Score the person's responses, following the same directions, and add up the total points for each section.

Empathy Assessment Completed by a Friend or Family Member

Student's Name:

Your relationship to the student:

Respond to the following statements using the number scale.

| 1 = Strongly disagree | 2 = Disagree | 3 = Slightly disagree | 4 = Slightly agree | 5 = Agree | 6 = Strongly agree |

1. Seeing someone who is upset makes this person upset.

| 1 | 2 | 3 | 4 | 5 | 6 |

2. This person tends to cry during sad movies.

| 1 | 2 | 3 | 4 | 5 | 6 |

3. This person thinks it's funny when others get teased and get upset about it.

| 1 | 2 | 3 | 4 | 5 | 6 |

4. This person gets upset when hearing about someone being mistreated.

| 1 | 2 | 3 | 4 | 5 | 6 |

5. When this person sees a homeless person on the side of the road asking for money, it makes him or her mad.

| 1 | 2 | 3 | 4 | 5 | 6 |

6. This person likes hearing about friends doing well in school even if he or she is not doing as well.

| 1 | 2 | 3 | 4 | 5 | 6 |

7. When someone gets mad at this person, he or she tries to understand why that person is mad.

| 1 | 2 | 3 | 4 | 5 | 6 |

8. When a friend complains about something this person thinks is trivial, he or she stops listening.

| 1 | 2 | 3 | 4 | 5 | 6 |

9. This person has a hard time listening to someone else's opinion without arguing when that opinion differs from his or hers.

| 1 | 2 | 3 | 4 | 5 | 6 |

10. This person can tell you the other person's main concerns even during the heat of an argument.

| 1 | 2 | 3 | 4 | 5 | 6 |

Reflection Questions

1. What is your reaction to how the other person scored you?
2. What did you learn about yourself by doing this exercise?

Worksheet 10.5: Listening Even When It's Hard to Do!

Name:

Think about a topic that you and a friend or family member have a strong disagreement about that you would be willing to discuss with that person. Ask that person to have a conversation with you about the topic and tell him or her that your job in this assignment is to practice empathy skills (reflective listening, asking good questions, understanding the other's perspective and emotions, and so on). Ask the person to stop you whenever you begin to argue your point rather than trying to understand his or her perspective. *Warning*: It may be hard for you not to argue your points!

Conversation Topic:

Person I talked with:

Rate yourself on how well you listened and tried to understand the other person. Rate yourself as a 2 if you show some elements of 1 and 3; rate yourself as a 4 if your answer shows some elements of 3 and 5.

Not effective		**Somewhat effective**		**Very effective**
Interrupted, argued own points		Listened some, some questions but some arguing my own points		Listened, summarized his or her view, asked open-ended questions
1	2	3	4	5

Ask the person you talked with to rate you on the following scale about how well you listened to and tried to understand his or her perspective (your grade will not be affected by the rating!).

Not effective		**Somewhat effective**		**Very effective**
Interrupted, argued his or her points		Listened some, some questions but some arguing his or her points		Listened, asked questions to better understand me and my views
1	2	3	4	5

Reflection Questions

1. How hard was it for you to resist the urge to argue your perspective? What did you do to help yourself concentrate on the other person's views?
2. What *new information* did you learn about the other person or why he or she holds the expressed opinion?
3. What benefit came from listening to and trying to understand the other person?

Worksheet 10.6: Self-Development Plan for Empathy

Name:

Part 1. Developing a Plan

1. Describe at least one way you will personally benefit if you increase your skill in developing empathy.

2. Choose two of the strategies listed in Appendix A for improving your empathy and write them here. Or come up with your own strategies. Identify the dates you will begin using your strategies.
    Date to begin:
    Strategy 1:

    Date to begin:
    Strategy 2:

Part 2. Outcomes of Your Plan

Complete this part two weeks after you have implemented your strategies.

1. Describe what happened when you began using these strategies. (If you never tried the strategies or gave up quickly, explain why you weren't motivated to give the strategies a chance to work.)

2. Do you think you will continue to use these strategies? Explain why or why not.

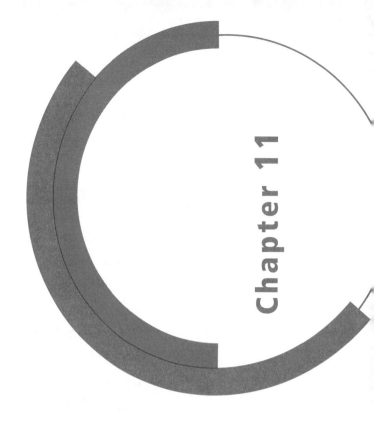

Chapter 11

Social Responsibility

Social responsibility comprises the desire and ability to willingly contribute to society, your social group, and generally to the welfare of others. This component of emotional intelligence involves acting in a responsible manner, even though you might not benefit personally.

— Stein and Book, 2011, p. 147

What is social responsibility? Acting in a collaborative, caring manner—even with those you may not know well and even when it may not directly benefit you—is the essence of social responsibility. Acting in a socially responsible way could range from volunteering to lead a major project to benefit your school to donating your time at a community service agency that provides shelter and food for the homeless. On a level closer to home, it includes simple things such as cleaning up after yourself so that others don't have to and doing your fair share of the work on a school project or family cleanup project. Socially responsible people think more about how they can help others, what they can do to make things better, and whether they are contributing in meaningful ways than they think about how they can minimize their contributions or save themselves time. Those who lack social responsibility sometimes take advantage of those who are more responsible—by not doing their fair share, waiting for someone else to clean up, or trying to avoid extra work.

WHY SOCIAL RESPONSIBILITY?

From the preceding description, you may think it sounds better to be less socially responsible because then you could get away with doing less work and have no feelings of responsibility for others' well-being. You'd have more time to do what you want, right? But doing more to help others increases your happiness, self-regard, and feelings of self-actualization (goal accomplishment and life satisfaction), so there are tangible benefits to being socially responsible. Also, consider this example of a college student who lacked social responsibility. He commented to friends that he made great grades in college and didn't have to do that much because the school he went to required almost all group projects, and he found that the females on a team were usually more than willing to do all of the work and still put his name on the project. So he "earned" excellent grades. While this may seem appealing to some of you, imagine this young man in his first career. When his boss asks him to do a complicated analysis or write a difficult report, will he have the skills and confidence to do it? It's doubtful. And there won't be anyone else whose grade depends on the quality or quantity of his work, so he alone will suffer the consequences from his earlier lack of social responsibility. Now imagine sharing an apartment with this guy. Will he be likely to unload the dishwasher, clean the bathroom, or vacuum? It's doubtful.

So again, why engage in social responsibility? Because the world will be a better place, you will get more joy out of life, and others around you will be appreciative of your contributions. And unlike the college student who slacked his way through, you'll develop skills and relationships that will enrich your life.

Behaviors That Demonstrate Effective Social Responsibility

- Engaging in volunteer work
- Serving on committees, joining clubs, or doing other things that benefit your school or community
- Thinking about ways to help rather than ways to avoid helping
- Taking out the trash or emptying the dishwasher at home when you see it needs to be done (not waiting to be asked to do it!)
- Doing your fair share on school projects

Behaviors That Demonstrate a Need to Develop Social Responsibility

- Coming up with reasons not to volunteer or help
- Looking the other way and avoiding making eye contact when someone asks for volunteers
- Failing to finish things you promised to do, leaving others to have to do them for you
- Not being bothered by others doing more of the work on a team project than you do; in fact, making that your goal!
- Failing to respond to emails, texts, or calls

Worksheet 11.1: Doing What's Right

Name:

The time is always right to do what is right.—Dr. Martin Luther King, Jr.

Fill out the following chart. When coming up with examples for each column, think about these five areas of your life: (1) group projects at school; (2) helping around the house; (3) helping or not helping a parent, partner, or friend with a very big task that will not directly benefit you; (4) volunteering your time for a good cause; and (5) volunteering to take on a project that would help your work group, a club, or team.

I demonstrated social responsibility when:	I did NOT demonstrate social responsibility when:
At school:	At school:
At home:	At home:
With a friend, family member, or partner:	With a friend, family member, or partner:
By volunteering for a good cause:	Turning down an opportunity to volunteer:
By volunteering to take on a project that would help my work group, a club, or team:	Not volunteering to take on a project that would help my work group, a club, or team:

Reflection Questions

1. Which of these experiences do you feel the best about and why?
2. Which of these experiences do you feel the worst about and why?
3. If you think you need to become more socially responsible, what will motivate you to do so? If you don't think you need to become more socially responsible, do you think others close to you would agree with that self-assessment? Explain your answer.

Worksheet 11.2: Cooperation

Name:

Go to the following YouTube clip, which features the song "Cooperation Makes It Happen" by the *Sesame Street* gang. (You probably watched *Sesame Street* as a kid and you may even remember this song, so just enjoy yourself!) http://www.youtube.com/watch?v=5exvfbnFMUg

Reflection Questions

1. Most of the characters were smiling much of the time they were working together. Why do you think there's an established research link between helping others and our own level of personal happiness?

2. *Sesame Street* is known for teaching valuable lessons to children. Think back to your childhood. What other individuals or groups taught you about working to help others, cooperating, or other aspects of social responsibility? What points did they stress?

3. If you could get everyone in the world (or your country, your school, or within your family or any other group you wish to choose) to cooperate about one issue, what would that issue be and how would everyone benefit?

Worksheet 11.3: A Company's Social Responsibility Policy

Name:

Look up the social responsibility policy for a company such as Microsoft, McDonald's, The Body Shop, Ben and Jerry's ice cream, or Timberland.

Company Name:

Social Responsibility Policy (if the policy is lengthy, write a one-paragraph summary):

Now pretend you are the president of a major organization. What are three things you would want your company to do to be more socially responsible?

Reflection Questions

1. Why did you pick the social responsibility areas you did for your company?
2. Some skeptics might believe the only reason some companies care about social responsibility is because it can help them increase sales. Suppose that assumption is true; would the company's behavior still be considered socially responsible? Explain.

Worksheet 11.4: My Social Responsibility Policy

Name:

Think about the area in which you are the least socially responsible from among the following areas: home/family; school; work; sports team, club, or organization.
Area chosen:

Write a social responsibility policy for yourself in this area. Make sure your policy addresses your current weaknesses in the area of social responsibility! When developing your policy, it might help to think about the following questions:

• *What* do I need to do more of or less of?

• *Who* would benefit from this and *how* would they benefit?

• *Why* did I pick this area?

• My social responsibility policy is:

Now share your policy with one person in the area you've chosen. It could be a parent, partner, teammate, coach, teacher, boss, or anyone else who is affected by your policy. Get them to sign your policy (or send an email indicating they have read it).

Signature of person reading your policy: _____

Reflection Questions

1. How much did you think about the challenges and costs of adhering to your policy when you wrote it? Why might this matter in your willingness to follow through?
2. What will motivate you to follow through with your policy?
3. How will others benefit from your policy?

Worksheet 11.5: Take Action!

Name:

Spend at least four hours doing something for someone else. You can volunteer at a local soup kitchen or after-school program, help build a Habitat for Humanity House, ask family members to give you four hours' worth of work to do that you normally would not do, pick up trash along the street, or whatever else you can think of.

Describe your activity:

Reflection Questions

1. Why did you pick this activity?
2. How did you feel during and after the activity?
3. Would you be willing to do this activity again? Why or why not?

The Student EQ Edge: Student Workbook

Worksheet 11.6: Self-Development Plan for Social Responsibility

Name:

Part 1. Developing a Plan

1. Describe at least one way you will personally benefit if you increase your skill in developing social responsibility.

2. Choose two of the strategies listed in Appendix A for improving social responsibility and write them here. Or come up with your own strategies. Identify the dates you will begin using your strategies.
    Date to begin:
    Strategy 1:

    Date to begin:
    Strategy 2:

Part 2. Outcomes of Your Plan

Complete this part two weeks after you have implemented your strategies.

1. Describe what happened when you began using these strategies. (If you never tried the strategies or gave up quickly, explain why you weren't motivated to give the strategies a chance to work.)

2. Do you think you will continue to use these strategies? Explain why or why not.

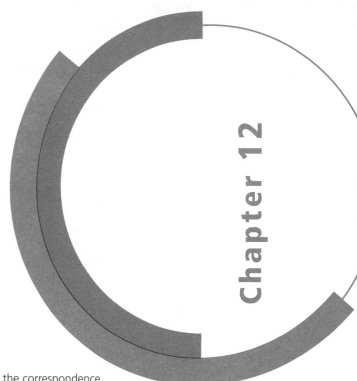

Reality Testing

Reality testing is the ability to assess the correspondence between what's experienced and what objectively exists . . . it is the capacity to see things objectively, the way they are, rather than the way we wish or fear them to be.

—Stein and Book, 2011, p. 159

What is reality testing? It is the ability to accurately read and understand environmental cues or factual information without exaggerating their importance or ignoring their relevance and value. People who lack reality testing are often surprised by events that others easily predicted. Take, for example, the case of a college student who enjoys science and has always wanted to be a medical doctor. This student, however, skips biology class regularly, has not kept track of his grades, and was late turning in a lab report. He expresses surprise when the professor tells him at midterm that he should consider dropping the course because he's likely to fail it unless his performance changes dramatically. How could that be? The student had failed to read the syllabus and did not realize that attendance would be factored into his grade; he also failed to look up his grades on tests and quizzes on the class website.

Contrast this student with a good friend of his who also aspires to go to medical school. Whenever this friend receives a

B on a test or paper, he becomes convinced that he will never get into medical school.

Both young men have poor reality testing skills, and both will suffer consequences. The first student will blithely ignore important cues, often leading to consequences that both surprise and harm him. The second student, in contrast, will exaggerate facts, leading to unnecessary worry and wasted emotional energy.

WHY REALITY TESTING?

If you want to be an effective decision maker, you must be able to discern facts, understand your environment, and objectively analyze situations, neither underreacting nor overreacting. If you lack this ability, you will make bad decisions, harm your relationships, and/or fail to perform as well as you could. Take, for example, the case of a first-year college male. He noticed a bulge under his armpit one day but just assumed it was a bug bite. Over the days and weeks, the bulge grew. When his buddies saw it one day while they were playing basketball, he shrugged off their questions and said he thought the bug bite had become infected. Several weeks later, when the student went home for a visit, his older brother saw the bulge and asked him whether he had seen a doctor. "No, not yet," he replied. Two days later a doctor delivered the bad news that multiple lymph nodes in his body were riddled with cancer. Only a massive dose of chemotherapy, followed by radiation and then surgery, could possibly save his life.

Yes, facts can sometimes be inconvenient, undesirable, and even terrifying, and situations can be filled with complexities, *but ignoring facts does not change the reality.* It only hurts our chances to emerge unscathed or to recover more quickly from whatever is happening.

Behaviors That Demonstrate Effective Reality Testing

- Asking questions or reading to gain information
- Paying attention to others' opinions when you are making a big decision
- Scanning the environment for information that might help you, keep you safe, or provide you with an advantage
- Being able to anticipate the consequences of choices

Behaviors That Demonstrate a Need to Develop Reality Testing

- Frequently experiencing surprise at how a situation turns out
- Tuning out others' questions or reactions
- Not seeking facts or information
- Ignoring facts or information you are provided with
- Not being aware of when you need to seek information
- Finding yourself constantly thinking about the worst that could happen in a situation
- Exaggerating possible consequences
- Worrying about things most people do not worry about
- Getting easily upset by situations that don't bother most people
- Not getting at all upset by situations that do bother most people

Worksheet 12.1: My Big Decision

Name:

1. Identify a big decision you will need to make in the next 6 to 12 months. Examples might include picking a college, deciding a major, determining whether to break up with a romantic partner, buying a car, moving to a new city to take a job, and so on. Describe this decision you are facing:

2. Now imagine your decision is like the funnel in the figure. At the beginning of the decision process, there's lots of information to consider and several, if not many, options. But as you answer the questions that follow, some decisions emerge as better options than others. Answer each question as thoroughly as possible.

Figure 12.1 The Information Funnel

- What information could I collect about this situation?

- What are the facts related to this situation?

- What are my opinions and assumptions about this situation?

- What would I like to do and why?

- Do the facts and information collected support what I would like to do? Explain.

Reflection Questions

1. If a friend were facing the same situation, what advice would you offer? Explain your answer.
2. What factors most influenced your decision? Are these factors more reality based (based on facts), fantasy based (based on what you'd like to see happen), or worry based (based on what you fear)?

The Student EQ Edge: Student Workbook

Worksheet 12.2: The Mirrors Around You

Name:

Answer the following questions about yourself using the numerical scores provided.

1 = Not at all like me

2 = A little bit like me

3 = Somewhat like me

4 = A lot like me

5 = Very much like me

_____1. I worry a lot about little things.

_____2. Others accuse me of exaggerating.

_____3. I imagine the worst.

_____4. I often realize that I've made too big of a deal about something.

_____5. I collect facts and information beyond what is needed to make a good decision.

_____6. I don't like to hear information that contradicts what I want to do.

_____7. I tend to ignore things I don't like to think about.

_____8. Others would describe me as unrealistic or idealistic.

_____9. I believe that my emotions should guide my decisions as much as facts should.

_____10. I'm often surprised at how a situation turns out.

Add your scores for items 1–5 and record that number here: _____

The higher your score for these questions (the range is 5–25), the more you tend to err toward being too focused on reality, too rigid in your perceptions, or too negative about possible outcomes.

Add your scores for items 6–10 and record that number here: _____

The higher your score for these questions (the range is 5–25), the more you tend to err toward being unaware of or uninterested in facts and reality.

Now ask your best friend or a family member to answer the same questions about you.

Student's name:

Your relationship to student:

Answer these questions about the student, using the numerical scores provided.
1 = Not at all like him or her
2 = A little bit like him or her
3 = Somewhat like him or her
4 = A lot like him or her
5 = Very much like him or her

_____1. This person worries a lot about little things.
_____2. Others think this person exaggerates.
_____3. This person imagines the worst.
_____4. This person often realizes that he/she made too big of a deal about something.
_____5. This person collects more facts and information than needed.
_____6. This person doesn't like to hear information that contradicts what he or she wants to do.
_____7. This person tends to ignore things he or she doesn't like to think about.
_____8. Others would describe this person as unrealistic or idealistic.
_____9. This person lets emotions guide decisions as much as facts do.
_____10. This person is often surprised at how a situation turns out.

Add your scores for items 1–5 and record that number here: _____
The higher the score for these questions (the range is 5–25), the more this person errs toward being too focused on reality, too rigid in perceptions, or too negative about possible outcomes.

Add your scores for items 6–10 and record that number here: _____
The higher the score for these questions (the range is 5–25), the more this person tends to err toward being unaware of or uninterested in facts and reality.

Reflection Questions

1. Compare and contrast how you see yourself with how the other person sees you.
2. Would you like to become more grounded in reality or more carefree in how you approach information and decisions? Explain your choice.

Worksheet 12.3: Failed Reality Testing

Name:

Choose one of the following two situations and conduct research about the decision made, what information should have been considered that wasn't, how emotions affected the decision-making process, and what consequences occurred because of the failure to test reality.

Situation 1. Launch of the Space Shuttle Challenger with school teacher Christa McAuliffe on board

http://www.heroism.org/class/1980/challenger.htm

http://ethics.tamu.edu/ethics/shuttle/shuttle1.htm

For even more information, check out Chapter 1 of *The Challenger Launch Decision: Risky Technology, Culture and Deviance at NASA* by Diane Vaughan, available through Google Books.

Situation 2. President Kennedy's decision to invade the Bay of Pigs

http://www.globalsecurity.org/intell/ops/bay-of-pigs.htm

http://www.probe.org/site/c.fdKEIMNsEoG/b.4221087/k.4551/JFK_and_Groupthink_Lessons_in_Decision_Making.htm

Answer the following questions about the situation you chose.

1. What information was available to the decision maker(s) that could have changed the decision?

2. Why did that information not influence the decision maker(s)? Was the information not shared, was the information ignored, or was there some other reason the information did not factor into the decision?

3. How did emotions play a role in the decision making?

4. What consequences occurred based on the decision?

Reflection Questions

1. Pretend you have to explain to a friend why emotional intelligence is often more important than IQ in determining success. Use the scenario you read to help you formulate your points.
2. Is there evidence in your scenario that people learned from their mistakes and improved their reality testing?

Worksheet 12.4: Decision-Making Interviews

Name:

Ask someone you know well to describe a very difficult decision he or she made. In the space provided, create interview questions for the person that will help you understand whether the person used good reality-testing skills or not. Make sure the questions will help you probe the person's reality-testing skills as part of the decision making.

Reflection Questions

1. Summarize what you learned in the interview.
2. Did the person use effective reality-testing skills or not? Explain your answer.

Worksheet 12.5: Reality-Testing Scenarios

Name:

Read the following scenarios and describe what effective reality testing would look like for a student in that situation. What information should the student seek? What facts should be considered? What questions should the student ask and to whom?

Scenario	Effective reality testing would include . . .
A student who is trying to get into a very prestigious college has signed up to take four Advanced Placement classes and two honors classes. She is also playing on a year-round soccer team and for her high school team. A week before school begins, she is approached by a teacher to become the editor of the school newspaper, which is published weekly.	
A Caucasian male university student is majoring in Arabic and international relations, preparing for a career working for the U.S. government in Arab-U.S. relations. His advisor mentions a summer study program in Iraq where the student could live in Baghdad with a sponsor family and interview locals about their feelings toward the United States.	
A college female is interested in pursuing a singing career. She learns about an opportunity to try out for a reality TV show that will feature musical talent. She is three months from graduation with a degree in accounting and has already been offered two well-paying jobs that would help her pay off some of her student loans. The singing competition would require her to drop out of school right now.	
A young professional has been passed over for a promotion. He's upset and makes an appointment with the boss to find out why.	

Reflection Questions

1. Pick one of the above scenarios and compare how you would have typically handled that situation to your response.
2. What are the short-term (and thus short-lived) benefits to not being effective at reality testing?

Worksheet 12.6: Self-Development Plan for Reality Testing

Name:

Part 1. Developing a Plan

1. Describe at least one way you will personally benefit if you increase your skill in developing reality testing.

2. Choose two of the strategies listed in Appendix A for improving reality testing and write them here. Or come up with your own strategies. Identify the dates you will begin using your strategies.

    Date to begin:

    Strategy 1:

    Date to begin:

    Strategy 2:

Part 2. Outcomes of Your Plan

Complete this part two weeks after you have implemented your strategies.

1. Describe what happened when you began using these strategies. (If you never tried the strategies or gave up quickly, explain why you weren't motivated to give the strategies a chance to work.)

2. Do you think you will continue to use these strategies? Explain why or why not.

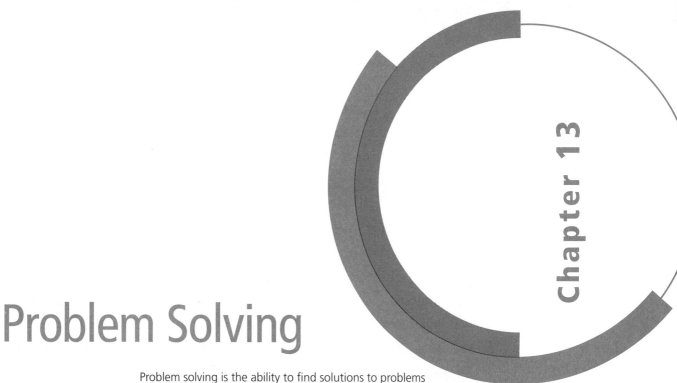

Chapter 13

Problem Solving

Problem solving is the ability to find solutions to problems
in situations where emotions are involved, and to understand how emotions
impact decision making.
—Stein and Book, 2011, p. 166

What is problem solving? Almost every day we solve some
kind of problem. Most, thankfully, are minor problems
such as fixing a jammed printer or finding our way to a new
location. But even a jammed printer can create major havoc
under certain circumstances. Imagine, for example, that you have
a paper due for your 8 ~AM class. You finish writing it at 1 ~AM
and are relieved but a little anxious because you know it's not your
best work. You press Ctrl+P. The first three pages print but then
the printer jams. You're already tired, and frustration comes
easily. You grab for the stuck piece of paper and pull. It tears.
You become more frustrated, grab another corner, and pull again.
It tears. You get more frustrated. You try to figure out how to take
the paper feed mechanism apart, but by now you're so frustrated
that you overlook the latch that allows you to open the printer.
And on it goes. The more frustrated you become, the less likely it
is that you'll solve this fairly simple problem in a timely way. If the
same problem had occurred at 1 ~PM and when you weren't tired
or feeling anxious, chances are you would have cleared the printer

jam much faster. The keys to effective problem solving are (1) to recognize that emotions affect our ability to solve problems and (2) to be able to leverage our emotions to help us solve problems rather than letting our emotions thwart us.

● WHY PROBLEM SOLVING?

How many problems do you confront on a daily basis? Now multiply that by 365. The need to engage in effective problem solving permeates our lives. Good problem solving includes the ability to frame the problem accurately and the ability to generate multiple solutions until we find one that works. But if emotions are involved and we fail to recognize them, our problem-solving ability can become impaired (in the EQ field, we sometimes say our problem-solving ability is "hijacked" by emotion), leaving us more frustrated and less likely to implement effective solutions. You don't need to read far in a history book to understand the importance of effective problem solving and the disastrous consequences of poor problem solving. Many Germans initially (and correctly) resisted Hitler's views. But as fear and a sense of helplessness to stop him permeated German society, the strongest opponents fled the country or became silent. Emotions, especially the more intense ones, can cloud our ability to understand the problem accurately and generate possible solutions. The consequences range from fairly minor (you print your paper on a computer at school) to severe (lives lost, families shattered in World War II).

Learning to adjust your emotions to fit the situation will greatly enhance your problem-solving skills. Did you know that if you want or need to engage in your best creative work, you should be in a very good mood? And, in contrast, if you need to engage in detail work, your mood should swing to the bad side. Why? People in good moods tend to overlook small things because their mood creates a sense of well-being that minor annoyances do not permeate. When we're not bogged down by minor matters, it frees our minds to be innovative. Likewise, a bad mood makes us more picky, more likely to be alert to possible problems.

Behaviors That Demonstrate Effective Problem Solving

- Stopping long enough to identify your emotion about the situation
- Understanding the root cause of the problem and why your emotions were triggered
- Generating multiple solutions with a clear head
- Mustering the best emotion to help you solve the problem
- Identifying the resources available to help you cope with or solve the problem
- Redirecting emotional energy that is hampering your ability to solve a problem
- Staying patient as you try different solutions

Behaviors That Demonstrate a Need to Develop Problem Solving

- Allowing your emotions to hijack you when you face a problem
- Not thinking about how emotions affect problem solving
- Being unaware of or unable to correctly identify the real issue in a problem situation
- Haphazardly trying different solutions (this is more likely to happen when emotions are overwhelming our ability to cope)
- Giving up—this is called *learned helplessness* and is often associated with a greater chance of becoming depressed

Worksheet 13.1: What Is My Emotion?

Name:

Identify which emotion is driving actions in the following situations and then come up with a way to change that emotion that would work for you if you were experiencing this situation.

- You and your dating partner attend universities 150 miles away from each other. You agree to take turns driving to see each other every other weekend. But when it's your partner's turn to drive, there's always a reason why *you* should drive that weekend instead. You spend lots of time texting back and forth, arguing about whose turn it is to drive.
  - What emotions would you be likely to experience if this was happening to you?

  - How would those emotions influence your problem-solving abilities?

  - Whose turn it is to drive is *not* the root problem in this scenario. What is the root problem?

  - What would your emotion be now that you've identified the root problem? How would that affect the way you are approaching this problem?

- Your parents give you spending money each month. In exchange, you are supposed to do some basic chores, such as walking the dog every day and cleaning your bathroom every week. That system works okay until school starts; then you're too busy to walk the dog daily. Your father points out, though, that you spend lots of time texting and playing computer games with friends. You tell your dad that everyone else in the family gets relaxation time and you should too. Your dad thinks you still have plenty of time to do your chores, keep up your grades, and relax. You dad tells you that he won't give you any more spending money until you do your chores.
  - What emotion are you likely to experience when your dad takes away your spending money?

  - Even if you did not say "angry" or "mad" (or something similar!) in response to the first question, pretend that you are mad. How would anger affect your ability to solve this disagreement with your dad?

  - What would you say if someone asked you what problem needs to be solved?

  - If your father was asked what problem needed to be solved, what would he say?

Reflection Questions

1. How would thinking about your emotions in these two scenarios help you problem solve more effectively?
2. Think about a situation in which you've had the same argument with the same person over and over. Explain that situation and identify at least one emotion you are experiencing that is interfering with your problem-solving ability. What could you do differently to solve the problem?

Worksheet 13.2: Failed Decisions Revisited

Name:

Go back to Worksheet 12.3. Reread the information about the *Challenger* explosion and then answer the following questions.

- What emotions were driving the following people who were involved in the decision to launch the *Challenger*? If their emotions changed during the decision-making process, note that. Explain how their emotions affected their ability to problem solve.
  - The engineers who tested the O ring

  - The engineering supervisor

  - Upper management at NASA who made the final decision to launch

- What problem do you think each of the groups was trying to solve?
  - The engineers who tested the O ring

  - The engineering supervisor

  - Upper management at NASA who made the final decision to launch

- Think about the stages of problem solving:
  a. Sensing that a problem exists and being confident and motivated to handle it
  b. Accurately and clearly defining the problem (that is, the real issue) and then collecting information about it
  c. Generating multiple solutions through brainstorming
  d. Weighing the pros and cons of each possible solution
  e. Choosing the best solution and implementing it

Write a two- to three-paragraph analysis of how the problem-solving process was applied when trying to decide whether to launch the *Challenger*. Note the points at which effective problem solving was and was not used. Identify which emotion or emotions drove the ill-fated decision to launch.

Worksheet 13.3: Solving Your Problems

Name:

Using the steps of problem solving noted in Worksheet 13.2, identify a problem you are having that you have been unable to solve. Then, in column 2, answer the question(s) about each problem-solving step. If you skipped a step or steps of the problem-solving process, leave that box empty. In column 3, identify the emotion you felt at each stage.

Steps of Problem Solving	Your Problem-Solving Steps	Emotion
1. Sensing that a problem exists and being motivated to fix it	What made you aware that a problem existed, and what did you do when you first became aware of it?	
2. Accurately defining the problem and collecting information about it	How did you define the problem?	
	What information did you collect?	
3. Generating multiple solutions through brainstorming	What possible solutions did you generate?	
4. Evaluating solutions	Briefly explain your analysis of each idea you generated in step #3.	
5. Choosing the best solution, implementing it, and assessing whether it worked	What did you do to solve the problem?	
	Did it work?	

Reflection Questions

1. Compare your answers to the steps for successful problem solving. Describe what is causing you the most difficulty.

2. How are your emotions affecting your problem-solving process? What emotion(s) might help you solve the problem more effectively?

Worksheet 13.4: But Can I Really Change My Emotion?

Name:

Remember, when we need to be creative in our work or problem-solving, it's best to be in a "good" mood because it frees us to be creative; when we need a lot of focus and attention to detail, it's best to be in a "bad" mood because it helps us be more critical. Read the scenarios described in column 1 and then complete the table according to the following instructions:

- In the second column, identify the typical or most likely emotion you would experience in that situation.
- In the third column, identify which emotion or emotions would be helpful to you in that situation.
- In the fourth column, identify what you would do to change your emotion.

Issue	Likely emotion	Helpful emotion	Strategy for changing your emotion
Coming up with an idea for your biology class project			
Looking over your three-hour mathematics final exam for errors after you completed the last problem			
Working under a tight deadline to finish the layout for the student newspaper			
Resolving a heated argument with your best friend			
Determining how to arrange all of your furniture in a very small room			

Reflection Questions

1. What can you do to remind yourself to examine your emotions when you are facing a problem?
2. Choose one of these five scenarios and describe the likely outcome if you let your typical or likely emotion influence you.

Worksheet 13.5: *One Fine Day*

Name:

Cue the movie *One Fine Day* to Scene 7, "Sammy at the Office," and watch through Scene 9, "Career Crisis." Previously in the movie, the parents had "problem solved" by each taking their child with them to work that day. Scenes 7–9 show how that decision worked out.

Reflection Questions

1. Analyze the emotions of George Clooney's character and Michelle Pfeiffer's character when they were trying to determine how to take care of the kids that day. How did their emotions influence their decision-making process?
2. Think about what you learned about reality testing in Chapter 12. Analyze their reality-testing skills in this situation.
3. Based on your analysis and what you've learned about problem solving and reality testing, would you expect their decision to work? Explain.

Worksheet 13.6: Self-Development Plan for Problem Solving

Name:

Part 1. Developing a Plan

1. Describe at least one way you will personally benefit if you increase your skill in developing problem solving.

2. Choose two of the strategies listed in Appendix A for improving problem solving and write them here. Or come up with your own strategies. Identify the dates you will begin using your strategies.
    Date to begin:
    Strategy 1:

    Date to begin:
    Strategy 2:

Part 2. Outcomes of Your Plan

Complete this part two weeks after you have implemented your strategies.

1. Describe what happened when you began using these strategies. (If you never tried the strategies or gave up quickly, explain why you weren't motivated to give the strategies a chance to work.)

2. Do you think you will continue to use these strategies? Explain why or why not.

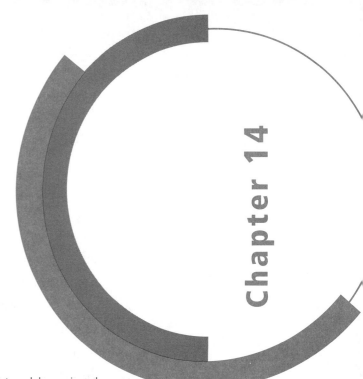

Chapter 14

Impulse Control

Impulse control is the ability to resist or delay an impulse,
drive, or temptation to act. Impulse control entails avoiding rash behaviors and
decision making, being composed, and able to put the brakes on angry, aggressive,
hostile, and irresponsible behavior.
—Stein and Book, 2011, p. 175

What is impulse control? Have you ever tried to go on a diet, work out more frequently, study on a regular schedule, pull yourself away from computer games or Facebook, spend less money on clothes, or not yell at your younger sibling who is irritating you? To do so, you needed impulse control. Controlling impulses means we can delay pleasure (study before partying, wait two more hours to eat, and so on), resist temptation (not yell even when we feel like it), and avoid rash behaviors (eating a whole box of donuts, spending $300 on a new phone that requires a new contract). Almost every decision we make involves the opportunity to either be impulsive or practice impulse control. You may not have considered it "making a decision" when you yelled at your younger sibling or partner. But it *was* a decision—just one that you did not take time to consider before you acted on impulse. It's probably not surprising to you that impulse control issues can be difficult to change. As with every other EI characteristic, you must first be aware of issues that challenge your impulse control, and then you must be willing to practice a calmer, more reasoned response. The effort will be worth it.

WHY IMPULSE CONTROL?

The failure to control impulses can sabotage relationships, cost you a promotion at work, get you kicked out of a class or off a sports team, or even cause a fatal accident. Teens and adults alike can overspend on credit cards, leading to years of pressure and poor credit ratings, or overeat or drink too much, leading to poor health and missed opportunities. The worker who yells at coworkers, fires off tempestuous emails, or blurts out frustrations in a meeting is unlikely to advance in the organization and in many cases is likely to be fired. Students can get kicked off a team, suspended from school, or placed on academic probation because of the failure to control impulses. The driver who engages in road rage may get too close to the car ahead and create a chain reaction of crashing cars. Effective impulse control does NOT mean you stuff your feelings, let others walk over you, never state your opinion, or never succumb to eating that piece of triple chocolate cake. Rather, effective impulse control—characterized by reflection about different options for actions and a willingness to delay gratification—will help you respond in a more measured way. So if you do eat that extra piece of the chocolate cake, you make up for it in the following days by eating more healthy foods and fewer calories.

Behaviors That Demonstrate Effective Impulse Control

- Weighing the pros and cons of decisions
- Being able to set a schedule and stick to it
- Getting work done before taking time to relax
- Speaking to others in a calm voice
- Setting a budget or spending limit and sticking to it
- Staying calm when stuck in traffic or waiting in a long line

Behaviors That Demonstrate a Need to Develop Impulse Control

- Feeding your cravings for food, alcohol, cigarettes, or drugs
- Overdrawing your bank account
- Playing or partying before studying
- Yelling at others
- Promising yourself you won't do [fill in the blank for you], but then doing it anyway
- Engaging in road rage behaviors
- Making rash decisions

Worksheet 14.1: Marshmallow Cravings

Name:

Go to http://www.youtube.com/watch?v=4y6R5boDqh4&feature=relmfu and watch the YouTube clip, "The Marshmallow Test." If this link is no longer active, search YouTube with the key phrase of "marshmallow study" and watch any clip related to this famous research.

Do you think having good impulse control as a child made a difference in these children's lives as a teenager? Justify your answer.

Children were followed into their teenage years and later as adults to determine the relationships among impulse control, academic and career success, social and emotional functioning, and coping skills. The following list contains results found during the teenage years (Shoda, Mischel, & Peake,1990). Children who were able to delay gratification and wait to eat two marshmallows exhibited the following advantages as teenagers:

- More adept at making social connections
- Less stubborn and more decisive
- Superior coping mechanisms
- Better grades
- Higher SAT scores

Pick two of these advantages and explain how better impulse control in a preschool child could be associated with such advantages as a teenager.

Reflection Questions

1. Do you think you would have eaten the marshmallow right away or waited so that you could have two marshmallows? Explain.
2. Take a position on the following statement: "Always exerting impulse control takes the fun and spontaneity out of life."

Worksheet 14.2: But I Want . . .

Name:

Pick an area in which you struggle with impulse control. Here are the likely categories: anger, impatience (for example, in traffic, waiting in line, waiting for something to happen), food, alcohol, cigarettes, drugs, partying before studying, computer use, TV watching, and anything else you can think of for which you find it hard not to react quickly or give in to temptation.

My impulse control challenge is:

When I don't control this impulse, the consequences usually are:

I find it harder to control this impulse when:

Here's what could motivate me to gain better control over this impulse:

Reflection Questions

1. What did you learn about yourself by doing this exercise?
2. How motivated are you to change your behavior related to this impulse?

Worksheet 14.3: *Survivor*

Name:

Watch an episode of the reality TV show *Survivor*. Pick a person on the show who has impulse control problems and answer the following questions. More than likely you will see issues with impatience or frustration or anger. If you cannot find an episode of *Survivor*, use the reality TV show *The Amazing Race*.

- What type of impulse control issue does this person have?

- How did the other people react to the lack of impulse control?

- Was the individual aware of the loss of control? If so, did he or she do anything to make amends? If not, how did the failure to acknowledge a problem affect the individual?

Reflection Question

If you were a contestant on *Survivor*, what issues or situations would be most likely to incite impulsive behaviors for you?

Worksheet 14.4: No Regrets?

Name:

Interview someone who will be honest with you about a time he or she engaged in one of his or her most impulsive behaviors and what the consequences were.

Relationship to me of the person I interviewed:

Age the person was at the time of the impulsive episode:

Question 1. Describe one of the most impulsive actions you have taken in your life.

Question 2. What were the consequences of your impulsive behavior? (Ask follow-up questions about relationships, physical and mental health, job performance, and happiness if the person does not mention these areas.)

Question 3. How has your life changed because of that issue? *or* What do you differently now as a result of that experience?

Reflection Questions

1. What was your reaction to hearing this person's story? What impact do you think this will have on you?
2. What was the individual's response to recalling this event?

Worksheet 14.5: Strategies for Success

Name:

Write down something constructive you could do in the following situations that would demonstrate impulse control.

- It's Saturday morning and you've just started working on a big project that's due Monday. A friend calls and asks you to do something you really enjoy that will take all Saturday afternoon.

- You're on a diet but are out with a group of friends and everyone else orders dessert.

- You're waiting in a long line at the movie theatre for a show that begins in five minutes. The person in front of you recognizes friends and invites them to cut in. They buy the last tickets for that show.

- Your cell phone plan is not due for renewal for three more months, but the newest iPhone just came out, and the features on it are much better than your current phone, which you've had for over a year. You go with a friend to look at the new iPhone. It's fantastic. She buys one.

- Someone walks into the room, picks up the TV remote, and changes the channel from the show you were watching.

Reflection Question

How likely are you to use the strategies you came up with? Explain your answer.

Worksheet 14.6: Self-Development Plan for Impulse Control

Name:

Part 1. Developing a Plan

1. Describe at least one way you will personally benefit if you increase your skill in developing impulse control.

2. Choose two of the strategies listed in Appendix A for improving impulse control and write them here. Or come up with your own strategies. Identify the dates you will begin using your strategies.
   Date to begin:
   Strategy 1:

   Date to begin:
   Strategy 2:

Part 2. Outcomes of Your Plan

Complete this part two weeks after you have implemented your strategies.
1. Describe what happened when you began using these strategies. (If you never tried the strategies or gave up quickly, explain why you weren't motivated to give the strategies a chance to work.)

2. Do you think you will continue to use these strategies? Explain why or why not.

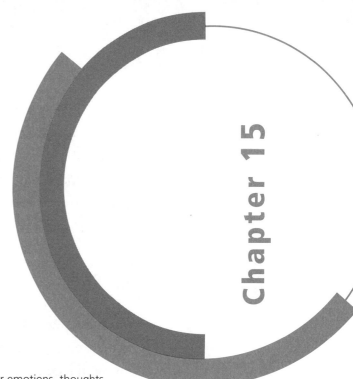

Flexibility

Flexibility is the ability to adjust your emotions, thoughts,
and behavior to changing situations and conditions. This component of emotional
intelligence applies to your overall ability to adapt to unfamiliar, unpredictable, and
dynamic circumstances.
—Stein and Book, 2011, p. 187

What is flexibility? It involves the ability to be deal effectively with (1) change that happens to you (for example, a teacher assigns a paper that wasn't on the syllabus, a friend cancels a weekend trip on Friday afternoon) and (2) change you need to initiate (for example, changing your college major because it no longer feels like the right fit). Flexible people cope better with both types of change, enabling them to be more skilled at managing their stress because they can adapt to a changing environment more readily than someone who is inflexible. Consider the following example: Your family decides to move your junior year in high school because of a terrific job offer your mother received in another city. Well-developed flexibility would enable you to adapt to the new high school and your new hometown—or you could be so inflexible that you immediately declare that you won't go, and if you're made to go, you'll be miserable and also make everyone else miserable. Emotionally you're holding yourself hostage and there's no way you will give the new city and new high school a fair chance. Being flexible does *not* mean that you have to be excited about or even agree with the decision to move; rather, it means that once the decision has been made, you can adapt emotionally and behaviorally so that you can excel and be happy in the new environment. Resisting the change will make the change even harder.

WHY FLEXIBILITY?

To understand why flexibility is so important, think about people who are now in their 50s and 60s. None of those individuals grew up with a computer, yet many of them *must* use a computer effectively in their professional lives. Most made the change. But some individuals in that age group refused to adapt to the changes required by computers. As a result, many of those people lost opportunities for promotions, created challenges for people they worked with (demanding phone calls instead of emails), or were given ultimatums to either learn to use a computer or get fired. It would have been much less stressful just to adapt to computer use in the beginning! Change happens with or without our consent and, sometimes, despite our loud objections. Fighting change, being fearful of it, or developing a reputation as being a rigid person will increase your stress and decrease your chances for success.

Behaviors That Demonstrate Flexibility

- Examining new information before reaching a conclusion
- Being willing to consider the possible advantages of situations or changes you don't like
- Hearing yourself say things like "We can try it that way," "Let's see what happens if we do XX," or "What do you need me to do differently?"
- Changing your behavior after making a mistake to ensure that you don't do it again
- Being open to feedback

Behaviors That Demonstrate a Need to Develop Flexibility

- Experiencing strong negative emotions when change happens
- Trying to talk people out of changes that affect you
- Getting nervous or anxious when you discover something different at home, work, or school
- Being unwilling to try something new
- Staying within your comfort zone of things you do well
- Having difficulty changing your mind

Worksheet 15.1: Reflections About Change

Name:

List the three biggest changes in your life so far (for example, parental divorce, getting fired, leaving home to attend a university, sibling with special needs, a new coach, changing schools, moving to a new city):

1.

2.

3.

Pick the change that was most difficult for you to adapt to and answer each of the reflection questions. (Suggestion: Focus on how the situation required you to show flexibility more than on the emotions you felt, such as sadness or fear.)

Reflection Questions

1. How did the change affect you?
2. What did you do to help yourself adapt to the change?
3. Looking back, how successful were you in demonstrating flexibility or adapting to the change? Explain why you were or were not able to adapt successfully.

Worksheet 15.2: Flexibility Survey

Name:

Answer each question below by circling the number for the response that most closely matches how you are, not how you would like to be.

Use the following scale:

Always or Almost Always	Usually	Sometimes	Occasionally	Rarely or Never
5	4	3	2	1

I get mad or nervous if a friend changes our plans at the last minute.

5   4   3   2   1

I get upset if I have to change my plans for the day.

5   4   3   2   1

When I eat out, I order the same items over and over.

5   4   3   2   1

I like to make decisions and then stick to them.

5   4   3   2   1

I get frustrated or upset when family members or roommates move furniture around.

5   4   3   2   1

I avoid trying new things.

5   4   3   2   1

I like to experience the same holiday rituals year after year.

5   4   3   2   1

It bothers me if someone puts my clothes away and doesn't follow the system I use for organizing them.

5   4   3   2   1

I have trouble shifting my attention from one priority to a different one.

5   4   3   2   1

Scoring Instructions: Assign these points to your answers:

5 Always or almost always = −5 (negative 5)

4 Usually = −3 (negative 3)

3 Sometimes = 0

2 Occasionally = +3

1 Rarely or never = +5

Scores below 0 (negative numbers) indicate you probably have some challenges with flexibility. Those close to 0 indicate you are neither flexible nor inflexible, and those well above 0 indicate you are flexible.

Reflection Questions

1. Are you surprised by your score? Explain why or why not.
2. If you asked the person who knows you best to answer the same items about you, how do you think your score might change? Explain.

Worksheet 15.3: The Price of Inflexibility

Name:

There are two possible ways you can complete this activity: (1) interview someone who is at least 60 years of age, using the following questions, or (2) conduct internet research and find events since 1950 that created the need for some flexibility if a person wanted to remain productive and happy.

Option 1

Interview someone who is at least 60 years of age. Ask that person these questions:

1. What is the biggest change that happened during your lifetime that affected you as an individual? Explain how you adapted to the change.

2. What is the biggest change that happened during your lifetime that affected you as a professional? (If the person was a stay-at-home parent, ask the following: What is the biggest change that affected how you parent?) Explain your answer and the impact of the change on you.

3. What is the biggest change in our society that has affected you personally? Explain how you adapted to that change.

4. Name one more change in any area of your life that caused you to make adaptations. How did you adjust to that change?

Reflection Questions

1. Would you characterize the person you interviewed as flexible, lacking flexibility, or somewhere in the middle? How has this person benefited or been harmed by his or her flexibility or lack thereof?

2. What was your reaction to being given options for this assignment? What does that indicate about your flexibility?

Option 2

Conduct internet research and find at least three major changes that have happened since 1950 that created the need for some flexibility if a person wanted to remain productive and happy.

1. List the three major areas of change. Describe how each required flexibility.

2. Which of these changes has had the most impact on American society? What would happen to someone who is inflexible, especially related to this change?

3. Which of these changes do you think you would have struggled with the most, given what you know about yourself right now? Explain.

4. Which of these changes would you have adapted to most easily, given what you know about yourself right now? Explain.

Reflection Questions

1. What is your reaction to the amount of change that has occurred since 1950? Explain your answer.
2. What was your reaction to being given options for this assignment? What does that indicate about your flexibility?

Worksheet 15.4: Stretching Yourself

Name:

Pick a routine that is very important to you, such as how your clothes are ordered in your closet, a daily trip to the nearest Starbucks, or what you do after getting home each day. For five days, do *not* engage in this routine. Answer the following questions:

Day 1: The routine I will stop as of today is:

What were your emotional and behavioral reactions to changing this routine?

Days 2–4: Have you been able to maintain this change in your routine?

If so, explain how you are feeling on day 4 about the change.

If not, and you reinitiated the routine, what caused you to do that? Explain.

Day 5: What were the benefits of changing this routine? Were there any consequences of changing this routine *other than* some nervousness on your part? If so, explain.

Reflection Question

Was changing a cherished routine harder or easier than you expected? Explain.

Worksheet 15.5: Flexibility Forecasting

Name:

There are many possible scenarios you could face as an adult that will require you to be flexible. For each scenario, write down your likely first reaction and then challenge yourself to see the benefits of flexibility.

Scenario 1. You have always spent the Thanksgiving holiday with your family. So has your fiancé. Your family homes are five hours apart, and both families have asked you to come for dinner on Thanksgiving Day.

My first reaction would be to . . .

One benefit to me of considering a different routine could be . . .

One thing I could say or do that would help me cope with this situation is . . .

Scenario 2. You are employed in your first job and have just gotten comfortable with your job responsibilities and your performance. Your boss approaches you about moving over to a different department where you will have to learn new skills. The pay and chances for promotion in the short term will be the same, but long term the move may have better opportunities. It's too soon to tell.

My first reaction would be . . .

One benefit to me of switching jobs could be . . .

One thing I could say (self-talk) or do to help me make this change is . . .

Scenario 3. You have been involved in a romantic relationship with someone for two years; you thought you would be together for the rest of your lives. Much of the excitement has evaporated from the relationship, but you know you both love each other. Unexpectedly, this person asks for some time away from you to think things over about the relationship.

My first reaction would be . . .

One benefit to me in this situation could be . . .

One thing I could say or do that would make this change easier would be . . .

Reflection Questions

1. Did you notice a common emotional or behavioral reaction in your initial responses to the changes? What does that tell you about your flexibility?
2. If these situations actually happened to you, would you be able to stop and think about the possible benefits of the change? Explain your answer.
3. What types of self-talk statements could you develop now that would help you cope with the need for change in the future?

Worksheet 15.6: Self-Development Plan for Flexibility

Name:

Part 1. Developing a Plan

1. Describe at least one way you will personally benefit if you increase your skill in developing flexibility.

2. Choose two of the strategies listed in Appendix A for improving flexibility and write them here. Or come up with your own strategies. Identify the dates you will begin using your strategies.
   Date to begin:
   Strategy 1:

   Date to begin:
   Strategy 2:

Part 2. Outcomes of Your Plan

Complete this part two weeks after you have implemented your strategies.

1. Describe what happened when you began using these strategies. (If you never tried the strategies or gave up quickly, explain why you weren't motivated to give the strategies a chance to work.)

2. Do you think you will continue to use these strategies? Explain why or why not.

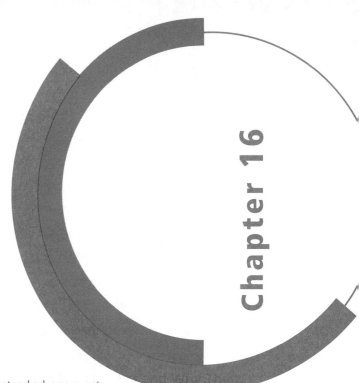

Chapter 16

Stress Tolerance

Stress tolerance is the ability to withstand adverse events
and stressful situations without developing physical or emotional symptoms,
by actively and positively coping with stress.
—Stein and Book, 2011, p. 196

What is stress tolerance? A famous stress researcher, Hans Selye, noted that the only way any of us can be free of stress is to die (Selye, 1976). Sounds extreme, right? Keep reading and you'll find out why that's actually a true statement. When thinking about stress tolerance, focus on the word "tolerance" rather than the word "stress." All of us experience stress every day of our lives, even as babies. Having a wet diaper, being too cold, and being hungry can be stressful to an infant. In fact, you'll notice, if you hang around infants long enough, that many of them develop self-soothing methods to cope with stress, such as sucking a pacifier or holding onto a soft blanket. All of us need to find ways to tolerate the stressors that come our way. There are several ways to improve your stress tolerance. First, you can redefine the stressor so that it is less threatening to you. Second, you can find ways to be less reactive to a particular stressor. And third, you can focus on your coping skills. All three of these will improve your ability to better tolerate stressors that you will inevitably face.

Many people don't realize it, but some of the most positive and exciting events in our lives are stressful. Going to college, graduating from college, getting married, buying your first house, and having a baby are some examples of "positive" stressors. How can such positive things be considered stressful? It's simple: those events create demands upon us, thus qualifying as potential stressors. The degree of stress you experience, though, may differ significantly from that of someone else going through the exact same event because that person either perceives the event differently (think of the student who never stresses over a test) or has different coping skills.

WHY STRESS TOLERANCE?

Feeling less agitated, coping with situations better, experiencing better health, and enjoying life more are just a few reasons you may want to improve your stress tolerance! Stress causes our body to release cortisol, a hormone that allows us to "fight" or "flee" in highly stressful situations. Our body releases some cortisol whenever we experience stress, whether it's a jammed printer, an upcoming test, or an overdue bill. Too much cortisol in our bodies, especially over long periods of time, will cause our bodies to begin to malfunction in some way. Maybe we start getting more headaches, get sick more frequently, cannot sleep, or constantly feel fatigued. Learning to cope with stress keeps our bodies healthy and our lives more enjoyable. So stop thinking about eliminating stress and start thinking about how to manage your stress.

Behaviors That Demonstrate Effective Stress Tolerance

- Being able to answer the question, "What stresses me the most?"
- Identifying a stress buildup before it becomes overwhelming
- Being able to calm yourself down by using self-talk, breathing exercises, or other simple strategies you can use in the moment
- Practicing specific coping methods on a regular basis
- Using available resources to help you minimize the impact of stress

Behaviors That Demonstrate a Need to Develop Stress Tolerance

- Frequently feeling agitated or on edge
- Overreacting to less significant stressors
- Being unable to calm yourself down when you're upset
- Using more destructive than constructive coping methods
- Becoming cognitively disorganized—having trouble concentrating, being forgetful, losing things

AN OVERVIEW OF THIS CHAPTER

This chapter is organized differently from the others in this *Student Workbook*. Each activity builds on the next, so even if you are not assigned each activity, completing all of them, in sequence, should help you learn to cope with stress more effectively. The primary of purpose of each activity is as follows:

16.1   Identify your biggest stressors
16.2   Understand why these issues stress you so much
16.3   Practice using the A-E model to minimize your stress
16.4   Take inventory of the ways you can cope with each of your stressors
16.5   Implement solutions

Worksheet 16.1: Identifying Your Stressors

Name:

There are two categories of stressors. Ongoing stressors have been causing you stress for more than a couple of days and are likely to continue. Daily hassles come and go, but when they happen, they can be quite frustrating. It can be hard to predict daily hassles, but we have included a few that most of us experience. Follow the directions for each column.

Ongoing Stressors	Daily Hassles
Rank order your top three ongoing stressors, with #1 being the stressor that causes you the most distress, #2 the second most stressful situation, and #3 the third most stressful. Add ongoing stressors you face if they are not included in this list.	Identify the top five stressors for you, not in terms of their frequency but rather in terms of how much stress they cause for you when they do happen. Rank order the top five daily hassles for you, with the top stressor as #1, the next most stressful #2, and so on. Add any daily hassles you face that are not included in this list.
____ money problems ____ family problems ____ problems with a romantic partner ____ health issues for you ____ health issues of a family member ____ separation from someone you love ____ social issues (feeling left out, no one to hang out with, being bullied) ____ team or group turmoil ____ pressure to succeed academically ____ pressure to succeed athletically ____ work problems ____ other: ____ other:	____ losing important documents because of computer problems ____ being late to an important meeting or class ____ jammed printer ____ no money to buy a meal and no time to go to an ATM machine ____ fight with a good friend, parent, or sibling ____ being embarrassed by a teacher or coach ____ being stuck in traffic for 10 minutes or longer ____ no good food to eat in the refrigerator ____ lots of work to do and not much time ____ spilled food on your white shirt and nothing else to change into ____ other: ____ other:

Reflection Question

What did you learn about yourself as you ranked each type of stressor?

Worksheet 16.2: Understanding Why You Get Stressed

Name:

Stress researchers have found that the degree of stress we experience is related to how threatened we feel by a particular stressor. Not everyone responds to the same stressor in the same way. For example, some students get very stressed out for big tests, whereas others barely notice any stress. One athlete may get very nervous before a big game or match, whereas another may feel less nervous. If you have been counting on getting an academic scholarship to a prestigious university, the pressure to succeed academically is likely to cause you much more stress than if you plan to attend a local university with open admissions. Likewise, having lots of homework and not much time may be more stressful if a prestigious university is your primary goal. The perceived potential for a stressor to keep us from attaining our goals is one factor in determining how stressful that event will be to us. One key to dealing with stressors is to identify how threatened we feel by that stressor.

Refer back to Worksheet 16.1 and list your top three stressors from each category. Write down how or why you feel threatened by this stressor.

Top Three Ongoing Stressors and Why They Threaten Me (keep me from meeting a goal, create extra work, and so on)	Top Three Daily Hassles and Why They Threaten Me
1.	1.
2.	2.
3.	3.

Reflection Question

What patterns do you see in terms of the things that threaten you? (Most of us will feel more threatened around key areas for us—such as academics, sports, or relationships—no matter what the individual stressor is.)

Worksheet 16.3: Irrational Thinking and Stress

Name:

Refer to Chapter 3 for a more detailed review of the A-E model, which explains how our *beliefs* about certain events are more important in determining our reactions than the event itself. In sum, here's the model:

A—the *activating* event (something that happens, something that needs to get done, a thought)

B—your irrational *belief* about the event (beliefs that exaggerate the importance of the issue, beliefs that contradict the facts, beliefs that exaggerate possible consequences, and so on)

C—the behavioral and emotional *consequences* of your irrational belief

D—*disputing* the irrational belief with evidence

E— the *effects* of disputing your irrational belief and replacing it with a rational belief

Pick one ongoing stressor and one daily stressor and analyze each using the A-E model.

Ongoing Stressor

A—the activating event; think about the last event related to this ongoing stressor

B—the irrational belief; what are you assuming or believing that is *not* supported by the facts

C—the consequences of your irrational belief; include both emotional and behavioral consequences

D—dispute the irrational belief with facts; substitute other possible beliefs

E—the effects, behavioral and emotional, of your new belief

Daily Stressor

A—the activating event; this is likely to be the daily hassle itself

B—the irrational belief; what you are assuming or believing that is *not* supported by the facts

C—the consequences of your irrational belief; include emotional and behavioral consequences

D—dispute the irrational belief with facts; substitute other possible beliefs

E—the effects, behavioral and emotional, of your new belief

Reflection Questions

1. Pretend you have to explain the benefits of using the A-E model to a friend. What would you say?
2. How will applying the A-E model make an event less stressful?

Worksheet 16.4: Resources for Coping

Name:

Coping with stress involves resources. Those resources may include time, forms of social support (friends, family, and mentors), money, skill sets, daily routines to minimize stress, resources at your school, help from professionals, and others. Refer back to Worksheet 16.1 and list your top three stressors from each category in the chart. Write down all of the resources you have that can help you cope more effectively with the stress. For example, if a chronic health issue is an ongoing stressor for you, your resources might include exercise, a special diet, professionals who can prescribe medicine or other forms of treatment, friends and family members who support you as you cope, and even your own ability to research your illness and possible treatments. If you're having trouble thinking of resources that can help you cope, ask a friend—this would be an example of using social support when stressed!

Top Three Ongoing Stressors	Top Three Daily Hassles
1. Resources I could use:	1. Resources I could use:
2. Resources:	2. Resources:
3. Resources:	3. Resources:

Reflection Questions

1. What resources could you develop that you are *not* using effectively now?
2. What would you have to do to develop these resources?

Worksheet 16.5: Stress Busters

Name:

In this activity, you will develop a specific strategy for dealing with your top three ongoing stressors. Stress busters will relieve and relax you, ensuring that you cope better with your ongoing stressors. Stress busters will not eliminate the stressor itself, but they will enable you to be less reactive to it. First, identify an ongoing stressor that you need relief from.

My ongoing stressor:

Now list three specific things you will do to cope better with this stress. (*Note*: Specific strategies are ones that someone else could observe you doing, so avoid vague strategies such as "I'll get less upset" or "I'll avoid the situation." Also, stress busters do *not* remove the stressor; they just help you to better cope with it. Some examples of stress busters include exercise, yoga, meditation, hobbies, pets, a walk outside, and reading.

1.

2.

3.

Reflection Questions

1. Are you willing to commit to these strategies? Why or why not?
2. What might get in your way if you try to implement these strategies?

Worksheet 16.6: Self-Development Plan for Stress Tolerance

Name:

Part 1. Developing a Plan

Coping with stress over the long term requires you to form habits now that will help minimize the effects of stress later. Rank with numbers the following coping strategies in the order in which you are willing to try them. For them to be most effective, you should aim to engage in the activity at least three or four times a week for a minimum of 30 minutes.

___ cardio exercise

___ meditation

___ yoga

___ sleeping at least eight hours a night during roughly the same time period each night

___ talking to a friend or family member about what bothers you

___ engaging in a hobby (reading, playing a sport, listening to music, and so on)

___ walking on the beach or in some other location that relaxes you)

___ playing with your pet

___ your own method for combating stress: _____

Pick at least the top two of the strategies you marked and, echoing the Nike slogan, just do it. Begin coping more effectively with stress right now!

Part 2. Outcomes of Your Plan

Complete this part two weeks after you have implemented your strategies.

1. Describe what happened when you began using these strategies. (If you never tried the strategies or gave up quickly, explain why you weren't motivated to give the strategies a chance to work.)

2. Do you think you will continue to use these strategies? Explain why or why not.

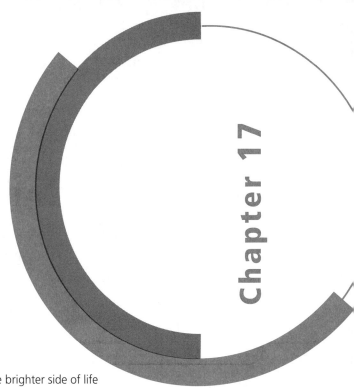

Optimism

Optimism is the ability to look at the brighter side of life
and to maintain a positive attitude even in the face of adversity.
—Stein and Book, 2011, p. 208

What is optimism? Most of you have heard the expression "seeing the glass half full" (or maybe you heard the "half empty" version!). This simple expression summarizes a key part of optimism: your perspective or how you choose to think about the situation. After all, the amount of water in a half-full glass is a *fact* that can be quantified down to the milliliter. But your perspective, or how you frame your reaction to this fact about the amount of water, has been learned over a lifetime. Are you someone who accentuates the positive, looks for the good in situations, and frames things in terms of how you could be successful? If so, you probably possess strong optimism. If not, you probably tend to be more pessimistic in your view of the world. The optimistic and pessimistic student will respond differently to most challenges. An optimist is likely to believe that a bad grade on a paper can be improved by seeking help from the writing center, talking with the professor, or writing more drafts of the paper, whereas the pessimist is likely to respond with a view of being stuck at that level or having a writing style that just doesn't appeal to that professor. Who is going to work harder on the next paper? And who has the best chance to improve his or her grade? In addition, the optimist is likely to be a more positive person because he or she focuses on possibilities instead of obstacles. It's emotionally draining to frame things more negatively, to believe that less is possible or that challenges are too difficult. But, lest you misunderstand, optimism does *not* involve engaging in magical thinking that everything will be perfect; rather, it means that you will remain positive and determined as you face challenges or problems.

● WHY OPTIMISM?

There are many reasons to develop your ability to be optimistic. Multiple studies over many years have proven the value of optimism in everything from recovering from a serious illness to being a more successful salesperson. The optimist who becomes ill believes that health can be improved and remains positive while seeking strategies and doctors who can help. This contrasts with the pessimist, who may frame the situation as "half empty," focusing more on the negative aspects of the illness and what hasn't worked, and losing hope and determination along the way.

    Martin Seligman, a famous researcher who has studied optimism extensively, once conducted what was supposed to be a classical conditioning study with dogs (Seligman & Maier, 1967). At first, dogs were placed in a box and bound so they could not escape. A bell rang and a shock followed. At first, the dogs tried to escape the shock. Seligman then removed the dogs from the box, waited a while, and placed them back in the box, except that this time escape would be easy—they were not restrained, they could see over a low fence, and all they had to do was jump out. But when the bell rang, they didn't move. Nor did they move when the shock started! Other dogs, which had never been restrained while receiving a shock, immediately jumped over the fence when the shock began. Seligman and others have termed the unmoving dogs' behavior—not escaping the shock even when they could—"learned helplessness." Pessimism and learned helplessness share many characteristics. First, the situation is framed negatively ("I can't escape"), which then affects behavior (giving up), which then exacerbates the emotional reaction (fear, anxiety, or depression). Other research by Seligman reveals that optimists live longer, have fewer illnesses, and experience more success (Seligman, 1991). Do you value those outcomes?

Things to Think About

1. Would you rather be around someone who talks about what is possible or who talks about what is impossible?

2. How do you react to negativity? Does it inspire you or drain you? What about positivity?

3. Think about a difficult challenge or problem you have faced, and answer the following questions:

   a. How did you frame the situation? Did you think more about the possible positive outcomes or the possible negative outcomes?

   b. What was your demeanor around others—did you project a positive attitude or a negative one?

   c. How long did you persist in solving the problem? Did you persist until things got better or you found a solution, or did you give up before that happened?

Behaviors That Demonstrate Effective Optimism

- Sticking with something until you solve it or get better at it
- Remaining positive even when you are facing difficult challenges
- Engaging in self-talk such as "I can do this" or "things will improve if I keep trying"
- Framing a situation in terms of what is possible or what benefits exist
- Believing that your effort or skill can make a difference in a situation
- Maintaining hope

Behaviors That Demonstrate a Need to Develop Optimism

- Giving up when things get hard or you are frustrated
- Focusing on what is wrong, bad, missing, or harmful
- Engaging in self-talk such as "This is hopeless" or "I can't" or "This won't do any good"
- Framing a situation in terms of what you could lose, what could go wrong, or why the solution won't work
- Believing you have no control over the situation

Worksheet 17.1: Optimism Begins with Framing

Name:

Suppose you come from a family with 12 children and that you are the seventh child born in the family. For each of the following scenarios, turn the pessimistic way of framing the situation into a more optimistic framing. In other words, think of the *advantages* of having 11 siblings!

I don't get much attention from my parents.
Reframe to . . .

I hardly ever get to buy new clothes.
Reframe to . . .

I don't get any privacy or time by myself.
Reframe to . . .

My family cannot afford to go on big vacations together.
Reframe to . . .

Reflection Questions

1. If you were from a 12-person family, it may be a *fact* that you would have to wear a lot of hand-me-down clothing. But that fact can be interpreted two ways: the pessimistic way (I don't get to buy new clothes) or the optimistic way (I have lots of choices of clothing and different styles). Try to think about *one fact* that you are currently framing either optimistically or pessimistically. Write the fact and your interpretation here.

2. How difficult was it for you to find an optimistic alternative for each statement? What does that tell you about yourself?

Worksheet 17.2: De-motivators—Watch Your Self-Talk

Activity developed by Dawn Dillon

Name:

The following is a list of pessimistic sayings that can be considered de-motivators. These quotes are intended to parody inspirational sayings that most of us have heard. These were taken from the website http://www.despair.com (retrieved July 10, 2010). Take each statement and change it from a pessimistic or deflating statement to an optimistic one.

I expected times like this. But I never thought they'd be so bad, so long, and so frequent.

When the winds of change blow hard enough, the most trivial things can turn into deadly projectiles.

The secret to success is knowing who to blame for your failures.

Dreams are like rainbows. Only idiots chase them.

Not all pain is gain.

At some point hanging in there just makes you look like an even bigger loser.

Hope may not be warranted at this point.

If it can make your job easier, it can probably make it irrelevant.

No single raindrop believes it is responsible for the flood.

If at first you don't succeed, failure may be your style.

Less is more. Unless you're standing next to the one with more. Then less just looks pathetic.

Hard work always pays off over time, but laziness pays off now.

Pressure can turn a lump of coal into a flawless diamond or an average person into an absolute basket case.

If you never try anything new, you'll miss out on life's great disappointments.

How can the future be so hard to predict when all of my worst fears keep coming true?

Reflection Questions

1. What sayings do you use to motivate you?
2. What negative sayings have you heard that you believe are true? How could you challenge those sayings?

Worksheet 17.3: Assessing Your Optimism

Name:

Directions for the Life Orientation Test—Revised

(Scheier, Carver, and Bridges, 1994)

Please be as honest and accurate as you can throughout. Try not to let your response to one statement influence your responses to other statements. There are no "correct" or "incorrect" answers. Answer according to your own feelings, rather than how you think "most people" would answer. Fill in the letter that best represents you in the blank space beside the item number.

A = I agree a lot.

B = I agree a little.

C = I neither agree nor disagree.

D = I *disagree* a little.

E = I *disagree* a lot.

_____ 1. In uncertain times, I usually expect the best.

_____ 2. It's easy for me to relax.

_____ 3. If something can go wrong for me, it will.

_____ 4. I'm always optimistic about my future.

_____ 5. I enjoy my friends a lot.

_____ 6. It's important for me to keep busy.

_____ 7. I hardly ever expect things to go my way.

_____ 8. I don't get upset too easily.

_____ 9. I rarely count on good things happening to me.

_____10. Overall, I expect more good things to happen to me than bad.

Score your results as follows:

Group 1: Add items 1, 4, and 10: A = 5, B = 4, C = 3, D = 2, E = 1
My total score for these items is:

Group 2: Add items 3, 7, and 9: A = 5, B = 4, C = 3, D = 2, E = 1
My total score for these items is:

Now, subtract your score for group 2 from your score for group 1. For example, if you scored 15 for group 1 and 10 for group 2, your score would equal +5; if you scored 10 for Group 1 and 15 for Group 2, your score would equal –5.

My overall score is:

Score Interpretations

A score of 0 means you are balanced in your tendency to be optimistic and pessimistic. A positive score, +1 to +12, indicates a trend toward optimism; the higher your score, the more optimistic you are. A negative score, ranging from –1 to –12, indicates more pessimism; the larger the negative number, the more pessimistic you are.

Reflection Questions

1. What is your reaction to your results? Explain.
2. What do you think were the most influential factors in your development of optimism or pessimism?

Worksheet 17.4: Pep Talks and Persistence

Name:

Take each of the following three scenarios and describe an optimistic response in terms of framing, self-talk, and persistence.

Scenario 1

You have been a starting member of the soccer team for two years. You are a senior, and a sophomore super-star has taken your place in the starting line-up.

- How can you frame this development to help you stay motivated?

- What things can you tell yourself to help you become the best soccer player you can be?

- How will you know whether you are persisting or have given up?

Scenario 2

You hope to get into graduate school in your field. You take the Graduate Record Exam (GRE) and score 100 points below what you need to score in order to get into a good school.

- How can you frame this development to help you stay motivated?

- What self-talk can you engage in to help you remain positive?

- How will you know whether you are persisting or have given up?

Scenario 3

You are graduating from your university in a year when the economy is bad. As a result, only 50 percent of graduates are getting a job that requires a bachelor's degree, 40 percent are working at a job that does not require a degree and 10 percent have not found a job at all.

- What things can you tell yourself to help you be motivated to improve your chances of getting a job that requires a college degree?

- Imagine that it is August after graduation in May and you still do not have a professional job.
    a. What would your self-talk be like if you were persisting?

    b. What behaviors would you be engaging in if you were persisting?

Reflection Question

Writing the above responses is much easier than living them. Who do you admire that you could seek motivation from? Explain how or why this person motivates you to remain persistent.

Worksheet 17.5: Perseverance Defined

Name:

Optimism does not guarantee us positive outcomes or getting what we want. What it does guarantee is that our journey, no matter what we confront, will be filled with hope, positive attitudes, and persistence. To see an example of optimism, go to http://www.chordomafoundation .org/perseverance-pledge/. Scroll down to the first paragraph and click on the phrase "powerful speech." Watch the speech by Justin Straus, a bright and loving young man who died from a devastating form of cancer when he was just 13 years old. (Justin's speech is preceded by a speech by his father who also displays optimism related to the family challenge of Justin's battle with cancer. The entire clip lasts about 15 minutes.)

Listen to Justin's speech for signs of optimism. Even though treatments for his cancer robbed him of energy and made participating in sports difficult, Justin never gave up. The defining moment of Justin's optimism occurred shortly before his death. He was hospitalized, unable to swallow, speak, or do basic self-care. Physical therapy, designed to keep his muscles strong while he was bedridden, exhausted him. Yet one day, upon returning Justin to his hospital room from physical therapy, the therapists tried to transfer him from the wheelchair to his bed. Although exhausted and weak from the effort he had put forth in physical therapy, he wanted to sit in the chair rather than lie in the bed. He motioned to the white board (which he used to communicate because he could no longer talk) and scrawled (he was also losing fine motor skills) the word "perseverance." (His actual handwriting is viewable if you click the link mentioned in the preceding paragraph.) Justin died just days after he scrawled "perseverance," but he never gave up, and as a result, his story has inspired many people.

Reflection Question

Justin was diagnosed at age seven. Optimism did not prevent his death, but it did help him cope with the illness and possibly extended his life longer than predicted. Listen to the speech and list at least three behaviors Justin engaged in that showed he was

- Remaining positive and hopeful
- Persisting in his efforts to fight the cancer

Worksheet 17.6: Self-Development Plan for Optimism

Name:

Part 1. Developing a Plan

1. Describe at least one way you will personally benefit if you increase your skill in developing optimism.

2. Choose two of the strategies listed in Appendix A for improving optimism and write them here. Or come up with your own strategies. Identify the dates you will begin using your strategies.

   Date to begin:

   Strategy 1:

   Date to begin:

   Strategy 2:

Part 2. Outcomes of Your Plan

Complete this part two weeks after you have implemented your strategies.

1. Describe what happened when you began using these strategies. (If you never tried the strategies or gave up quickly, explain why you weren't motivated to give the strategies a chance to work.)

2. Do you think you will continue to use these strategies? Explain why or why not.

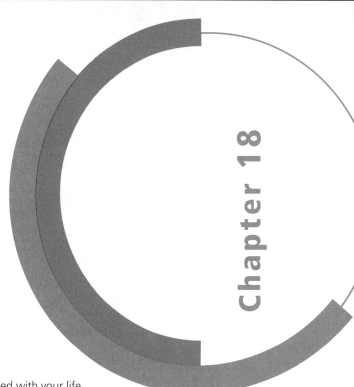

Happiness

Happiness is the ability to feel satisfied with your life,
to enjoy yourself and others, and to have fun.
—Stein and Book, 2011, p. 219

What is happiness? Believe it or not, happiness can be a slippery concept to define—much less to recognize that you are feeling. If asked about times in your life when you were the happiest, you can probably conjure up images of big moments, exciting events, or strong connections with people you care about. Day-to-day happiness, though, is determined by other things, and it comes from within us more than being driven by external events. Don't misunderstand: some external events are devastating enough to cause unhappiness that can last for years. Yet even in those cases—such as death of a parent, partner, or child; a chronic and serious health problem; or severe poverty—you will always find some people who manage to be happier than others who are facing the exact same circumstances. The opposite is also true. Lottery winners who have become instant millionaires are giddy with joy the day they find out, but one year later, they are no happier than they were previous to winning the lottery. How can that be? Again, your happiness largely comes from within you. In fact, several of the other emotional intelligence scales that we've studied throughout this book contribute to your happiness levels. It's easier to be happy when you set and achieve meaningful goals (self-actualization), connect with other people in meaningful ways (interpersonal relationship), accept yourself as you are but still strive for improvement (self-regard), and face challenging situations with a sense of hope and determination (optimism). So don't count on things, possessions, or events to make you happy. Although they provide temporary joy, things and events pale in comparison to what's going on inside of us and the kinds of relationships we have with others.

WHY HAPPINESS?

Why happiness? This probably seems like a very silly question. Why not? Who would choose the feelings of sadness or even despair that accompany a lack of happiness? But there's more to happiness than our internal feelings of well-being. Happier people also experience many other benefits, such as attracting friends and enjoying life. Because they exude cheerfulness, happy people make others around them more cheerful, with each person reinforcing the other's happiness. You can probably imagine how much easier it is to set goals and work hard to achieve them or to face adversity with a positive attitude if you are beginning from a point of happiness. Happiness in effect reinforces itself, making it easier for us to engage in the things that promote happiness and therefore ensuring that we remain happy.

Behaviors That Demonstrate Happiness

- Laughing and smiling frequently
- Engaging in activities you find meaningful
- Engaging in relationships that give you joy
- Understanding what puts you in a bad mood or good mood and doing things that enhance your mood
- Engaging in positive rather than negative self-talk

Behaviors That Demonstrate a Need to Develop Happiness

- Preferring to be alone most of the time
- Avoiding meaningful relationships
- Getting into a bad mood and staying there
- Finding very little that you can laugh about
- Not feeling good about yourself
- Surrounding yourself with others who complain or are negative or critical
- Not having goals that give you pleasure

A NOTE ABOUT DEPRESSION

Depression occurs when there is a biological imbalance in neurotransmitters responsible for elevating mood. If you are suffering from clinical depression, most of the exercises that follow will not make a significant difference in your happiness level until you find ways to correct the neurotransmitter imbalance. Medication (antidepressants), counseling, exercise, meditation, and special diets can all help combat depression. Depression can range from mild to severe. Symptoms of depression include: depressed mood with few or no upbeat periods, irritability, sadness, feelings of worthlessness, changes in appetite or sleep, and, in more severe cases, thoughts of suicide. Seek help from a counselor, psychologist, or school official if you think you need to be evaluated for depression.

Worksheet 18.1: Taking Stock of Your Happiness Level

Name:

Martin Seligman and colleagues at the University of Pennsylvania have done a lot of research about happiness, optimism, and positive psychology (see, for example, Seligman, 1991, and Seligman & Maier,1967). Go to http://www.authentichappiness.sas.upenn.edu/default.aspx and create an account (it's free!) by signing in with a username and password. You will be asked a few questions about yourself. Then complete the Fordyce Current Happiness survey and the General Happiness Questionnaire. Either print out your results or write down how you compare to others your age and on one of the other key comparisons (for example, your zip code).

Reflection Questions

1. Are your current happiness levels (Fordyce) and enduring happiness levels (General Happiness Questionnaire) about the same—that is, within 10 percent?
   a. If not, what is creating the difference?
   b. If so, what elements of your life contribute to both your current and your enduring happiness?
2. What is your reaction to how you compared with others completing the same survey?

Worksheet 18.2: Laugh a Little, Laugh a Lot

Name:

Access at least one of the following YouTube clips. (If these are not available, put the words "baby laughing" or "infant laughing" in the YouTube search box).

Baby Laughing Hysterically at Ripping Paper (original), http://www.youtube.com/watch?v= RP4abiHdQpc&feature=related

Laughing Quadruplets—The Next Day, http://www.youtube.com/watch?v=zZH0sNsaAz4&feature=related

Reflection Questions

1. Most of us will laugh as we watch these videos. What does that tell you about the power of positive emotions?

2. The term "emotional contagion" has been used to describe how our moods are affected by others' moods, both negatively and positively.

   a. Think of someone in your life who provides you with positive emotional contagion. Write his or her name or initials here:

      How does your mood and behavior usually change when you are around this person?

   b. Think of the most negative person you have to interact with regularly. Write his or her initials or something to help you remember who that person is here:

      How does this person affect your mood and behavior?

   c. In general, what do you think your level of positive emotional contagion is? Explain.

Worksheet 18.3: Does Money Buy Happiness?

Name:

1. Most of us have heard the saying "Money can't buy happiness." Choose one of the following areas and do research about the relationship between this area and happiness (follow your instructor's guidelines for acceptable sources for your research).
   * Money (including wealth and poverty)
   * Religion
   * Married versus single
   * Health
   * Use of social media
2. Write a brief summary of what you found:

3. List your sources of information here (journal article title, book title, internet link, and so on):

Reflection Question

What finding surprised you the most? Explain why this surprised you.

Worksheet 18.4: Well-Being Indicators

Name:

Several EI factors are associated with a greater likelihood of being happy. Four have been addressed in previous chapters in this workbook: self-regard, self-actualization, interpersonal relationships, and optimism. Look back at the definitions of each of these characteristics in the previous chapters and then fill in the right-hand column of the following table.

Emotional Intelligence Area	Relationship to Happiness	One Strength; One Improvement
Self-Regard	The ability to accept and love ourselves as we are, even while striving to improve, enables us to feel positive about ourselves. Being too self-critical inhibits happiness.	1. Name one area of your life in which you have high self-regard: 2. Describe one area of your life (for example, academic confidence, body image, social interactions, athletic skills) in which your self-regard needs to improve and one strategy for how you could make improvements. Area: Improvement Strategy:
Self-Actualization	The ability to realize our potential begins with being involved in activities that we find meaningful and fulfilling. Self-actualized people are excited about their pursuits and try to do their best.	1. Name an area of your life in which you experience excitement, meaning, and fulfillment: 2. Describe one strategy for how you could improve your self-actualization in another area of your life:

Interpersonal Relationships	Social support is associated with a stronger sense of well-being. All of us need to feel connected to others in meaningful ways.	1. Name one friendship or relationship that gives your life meaning and happiness: 2. Describe one strategy that you could use to improve other interpersonal relationships in your life:
Optimism	All of us face obstacles and adversity. The ability to remain positive, to keep trying, and to believe we will eventually succeed is critical to feeling happy.	1. Name one time (or one area of your life) when (where) you felt optimistic: 2. Describe one strategy that you could use to improve your optimism:

Worksheet 18.5: *The Pursuit of Happyness*

Name:

Access the following YouTube clips from the movie *The Pursuit of Happyness,* starring Will Smith. Explain how each of the clips relates to one or more of the four indicators of well-being covered in Worksheet 18.4. The relevant dimensions are listed in parenthesis after the clip.

- Basketball Dreams, http://www.youtube.com/watch?v=NyNyNphyIYU&feature=related (self-regard, self-actualization)
- The Time Machine and Dinosaurs, http://www.youtube.com/watch?v=Joaqf393lt0 (interpersonal relationships, optimism)
- Cold Calls, http://www.youtube.com/watch?v=emzARZsJntw (optimism, self-actualization)
- Job Offer, http://www.youtube.com/watch?v=U8uWmzLydsI&feature=related (self-actualization, interpersonal relationships)

Reflection Questions

1. Self-regard: How does Will Smith's character teach his son about self-regard? How does he show his own self-regard?
2. Self-actualization: What goals is Will Smith's character pursuing? What things give his life meaning and fulfillment?
3. Interpersonal relationships: What evidence is there of a strong interpersonal relationship with his son? How does he create mutuality and connection with someone so much younger?
4. Optimism: How does Will Smith's character display optimism? At what points might someone else have given up?

Worksheet 18.6: One Commitment—Self-Development Plan for Happiness

Name:

What is one behavior that you will commit to begin practicing today and continue until it becomes a regular part of your life that you know will positively influence your happiness? Remember, the fastest way to increase happiness is to improve your skills in one of the areas related to happiness: self-regard, self-actualization, interpersonal relationship, and optimism. Look at the strategies in Appendix A for these four subscales.

Identify one behavior you will begin practicing today that will improve your happiness:

Insert a reminder message into your phone or calendar for six months from today that prompts you to answer the following question: Did you follow through on your one commitment to happiness?

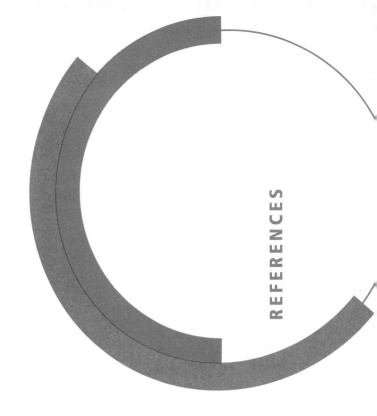

Ellis, A. (2004). Expanding the ABCs of rational emotive therapy. In A. Freeman, M. J. Mahoney, P. Devito, & D. Martin (Eds.), *Cognition and Psychotherapy* (2nd ed., pp. 185–196). New York: Springer.

Mann, D., & Kanoy, K. (2010, February). *The EQ factor in student retention and success: From theory to practice.* Paper presented at the annual First Year Experience Conference, Denver, CO.

Pascarella, E. T., & Terenzini, P. T. (2005). *How college affects students.* San Francisco: Jossey-Bass.

Rotter, J. (1966). Generalized expectancies for internal versus external control of reinforcement. *Psychological Monographs, 80,* 609.

Scheier, M. F., Carver, C. S., & Bridges, M. W. (1994). Distinguishing optimism from neuroticism (and trait anxiety, self-mastery, and self-esteem): A re-evaluation of the Life Orientation Test. *Journal of Personality and Social Psychology*, 67, 1063–1078.

Schulman, P. (1995). Explanatory style and achievement in school and work. In G. Buchanan & M. Seligman (Eds.), *Explanatory style* (pp. 159–171). Hillsdale, NJ: Lawrence Erlbaum.

Seligman, M. E. P., & Maier, S. F. (1967). Failure to escape traumatic shock. *Journal of Experimental Psychology, 74*(1), 1–9.

Seligman, M. (1991). *Learned optimism: How to change your mind and your life.* New York: Knopf.

Selye, H. (1976). *The stress of life.* New York: McGraw-Hill.

Shivpuri, S., & Kim, B. (2004, Fall). Do employers and colleges see eye to eye? *College Student Development and Assessment,* 37–44.

Shoda, Y., Mischel, W., & Peake, P. (1990). Predicting adolescent cognitive and self-regulatory competencies from preschool delay of gratification: Identifying diagnostic conditions. *Developmental Psychology, 26*(6), 978–986.

Sparkman, L. (2009). Emotional intelligence as a non-traditional predictor of college-student retention and grades. *Dissertation Abstracts International: Section A. Humanities and Social Sciences, 69*(8), 3068.

Stein, S., Book, H., & Kanoy, K. (2013) *The student EQ edge: Emotional intelligence and your academic and personal success.* San Francisco: Jossey-Bass.

Stein, S., & Book, H. (2011). *The EQ edge: Emotional intelligence and your success.* Ontario: Wiley.

YouTube Reference List

Baby Laughing Hysterically at Ripping Paper. (2011, January 24). [Video file]. Retrieved from http://www.youtube.com/watch?v=RP4abiHdQpc&feature=related

CBS News. (2010, April 21). The marshmallow test [Video file]. Retrieved from http://www.youtube.com/watch?v=4y6R5boDqh4&feature=relmfu

The Centre for Confidence and Well-being. (2008, April 24). Assertiveness scenarios: 10 examples [Video file]. Retrieved from http://www.youtube.com/watch?v=Ymm86c6DAF4

Fox Sports. (2011, November 24). Ndamukong Suh Stomp ejection from Thanks giving day game [Video file]. Retrieved from http://www.youtube.com/watch?v=ZXDmCVSnn1U

Little, Ryan (Director). (2005, March 25). *Saints and Soldiers*: Sharing secrets [Video file]. Retrieved from http://www.youtube.com/watch?v=2XkLOT9J1vs&feature=fvst

Mathias, S. (2010, August 25). Laughing quadruplets—The next day [Video file]. Retrieved from http://www.youtube.com/watch?v=zZH0sNsaAz4&feature=related

Mucino, Gabriele (Director). (2006, December 15). *The Pursuit of Happyness*—Protect your dreams [Video file]. Retrieved from http://www.youtube.com/watch?v=NyNyNphyIYU&feature=related

Mucino, Gabriele (Director). (2006, December 15). *The Pursuit of Happyness*—Dinosaurs [Video file]. Retrieved from http://www.youtube.com/watch?v=JOaqf393It0

Mucino, Gabriele (Director). (2006, December 15). *The Pursuit of Happyness*—Cold calling [Video file]. Retrieved from http://www.youtube.com/watch?v=emzARZsJntw

Mucino, Gabriele (Director). (2006, December 15). *The Pursuit of Happyness*—Final scene [Video file]. Retrieved from http://www.youtube.com/watch?v=U8uWmzLydsI&feature=related

Public Broadcasting System. (2008, February 17). *Sesame Street*—"Cooperation makes it happen" [Video file]. Retrieved from http://www.youtube.com/watch?v=5exvfbnFMUg

WGN-TV Chicago. (2010, February 18). Helicopter parents: The lengths parents go to pamper and please their kids [Video file]. Retrieved from http://www.youtube.com/watch?v=ufEfeDP7vBA&feature=related

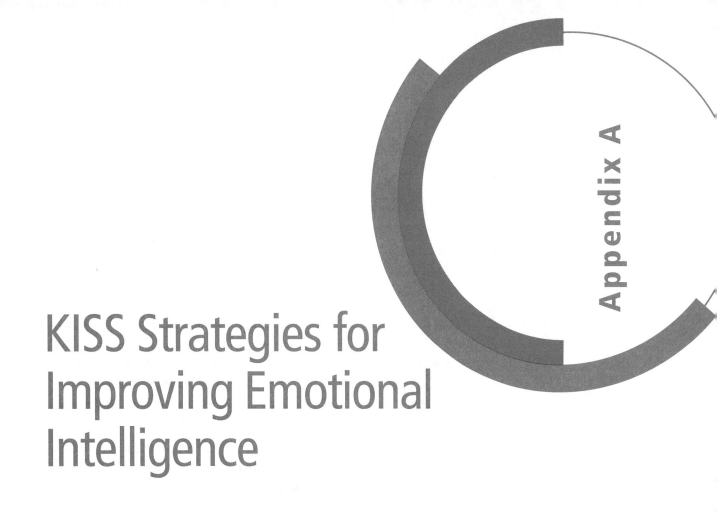

KISS Strategies for Improving Emotional Intelligence

This chart presents over 60 strategies for Keeping It Simple and Specific (KISS).

Self-Perception Realm

Emotional Self-Awareness	1. Make a list of values important to you (examples: honesty, respect, fairness, spontaneity) that, when violated, tend to push your "hot buttons." 2. Make a list of people who tend to push your hot buttons. Identify which of your important values that they tend to violate or what they do to push your hot buttons. 3. Use a daily log to record the three most significant emotional events of each day. Write down the emotion word (mad, sad, glad, scared, anxious), what triggered it (interaction with someone, value being violated, thoughts you had, text you received), and how you responded internally and externally. Note: You may end up writing down the same emotion word three times.

(continued)

	4. Set a timer on your watch or iPhone for every 30, 45, or 60 minutes for a three-day period. Write down your mood (positive, neutral, negative) each time the timer goes off and what emotion, if any, you are experiencing. Identify what caused the emotion (person, hot button issue, assignment, and so on) and thus the mood. 5. Look over the daily logs you kept for strategies 3 or 4 or both. What patterns do you notice with your emotions? Are most of your emotions positive or negative? Explain why you think the pattern occurs.
Self-Regard	6. Write down your three greatest strengths and your three areas where the greatest development is needed. Have two close friends or family members do the same and give them permission to be honest. Compare where your lists differ. Do others see you as you see yourself? 7. Use positive self-talk, such as "I have accomplished similar tasks before," "I have practiced hard and have improved," or "I know others I can call on to help me accomplish this task." 8. Think of something that bothers you frequently. Challenge negative thinking you might be experiencing by using the A-E model found in Chapter 3. 9. Share three of your goals with others. Get them to comment on whether goals you set are realistic within the time frame in which you will pursue them. If not, revise them. 10. Tape a list of your three greatest strengths to your desk or mirror, or type them into your phone. When in difficult situations, make sure to draw on these strengths. 11. Identify one thing you'd like to change about yourself. Write down one strategy that you can practice daily to foster this change. (Example: Change your tendency to dominate a conversation by asking three questions before you make a comment.)
Self-Actualization	12. Think about the current school assignments or content you most enjoy. What college majors or careers could you pursue that match with these skills and interests? 13. Identify a challenging academic goal. How will you feel if you accomplish this goal? 14. Identify two goals for school that are *unrelated* to grades. Why are these goals important to you?

	15. For assigned tasks you do not find fulfilling but are necessary (or required by a professor), assign a specific time period to work on that task each day or week and stick to the schedule. 16. If there are extreme mismatches between the academic subjects you most enjoy (for example, math) and the courses you are required to take (for example, English, foreign language, history, biology), list three reasons you might benefit from taking these other courses.

Self-Expression Realm

Emotional Expression	17. Listen to yourself—do you say "You make me feel" when you mean "I feel"? Take ownership of your feelings by saying "I feel . . ." 18. Practice using "I" messages when you are experiencing a strong emotion. "I feel *[insert emotion word]* because *[describe facts only!]*, and the effect on me is _____." (Example: "I am frustrated because you did not complete your part of the project on time and the effect on me is that my grade will suffer.") 19. Identify three situations that trigger different emotions. Write down how you could express your emotions and whom you would express them to for each situation. Use "I" messages to express yourself! 20. Pay attention to your body language. Do you have your arms folded? Are you leaning back? Are you frowning or glaring? Are you smiling and nodding? Your nonverbal expressions of emotion are *more* indicative of your feelings than your verbal expressions, so pay attention to what you are communicating nonverbally. Schedule a check-in by setting your cell phone to buzz three times a day; when it buzzes, ask someone around you what kind of nonverbal cues you were giving off at the time. 21. Give a friend, family member, or classmate permission to point out when you are displaying emotion nonverbally but not verbally. Write down what they observed, what triggered your emotion, and what you could have said.

(continued)

Independence	22.	Think about the last team project you participated in. Answer the following questions and then analyze whether your level of independence is too high (never want to work with others) or too low (cannot work without others' support or approval).
		• Did I take over someone else's tasks to avoid a meeting?
		• Did I refuse a request for meetings because I prefer to work alone?
		• Did I ask someone else for help on work I was supposed to do by myself?
		• Did I go to others to clarify instructions or ask their opinions of what I should do?
	23.	If you tend to be too independent (prefer working alone), ask someone else to complete a task you could do by yourself and ask for a meeting to review the results.
	24.	If you tend to be too dependent (prefer getting clearance from others before proceeding), identify one task to complete by yourself with no extra support from others.
	25.	Make a decision by yourself that typically you would let someone else make or first get their approval for.
	26.	Go somewhere by yourself or do something by yourself that you normally would not do alone.
Assertiveness	27.	Write down the most recent time you did not express a thought, belief, opinion, or feeling that was important to you in a face-to-face group setting. Identify the reason for your silence and what consequences occurred as a result of your silence. (For example, maybe you were scared to be honest with someone and ended up feeling frustrated by not sharing your opinion, or maybe you had to implement a plan you disagreed with.)
	28.	Write down one piece of reasonable constructive criticism to give your friend, coach, teacher, or family member. (Put the comment in "I" message format.) Then deliver the message.
	29.	Write down assertive messages you wish to deliver before stating them out loud. Practice, if necessary, and then deliver the message!
	30.	Watch the facial expressions of others after you deliver an assertive message. Were their expressions positive, neutral, or negative? What about their actions?

	31.	Ask three others whom you trust and who will be honest whether you tend to be too aggressive (hurt others while trying to be assertive) or too passive (fail to state your opinions or feelings often enough). Ask for specific examples. Then practice responding differently (more assertive, less aggressive or passive) the next time you face this situation.

Interpersonal Realm

Interpersonal Relationship	32.	If you tend to be a high achiever who studies a lot, schedule weekend or evening time to go out, get on Facebook, or do something else social.
	33.	Join clubs or groups that interest you. Participate in their activities outside of meeting time.
	34.	Plan something fun and invite others to go along.
	35.	Learn how to scaffold your interactions: • With someone you recognize but do not know, sit at the same table in the cafeteria and start a conversation about what classes that person is taking, campus activities, sports events, or any other topic you would be likely to have in common. • For someone you already know but who is not a good friend, talk about a common area of interest (a sport you both play, an assignment in one of your classes, or a common friend). • Think of something you can tell a good friend that you have not shared with that person yet.
Empathy	36.	Develop a list of neutral questions or statements that you can use in a variety of situations to elicit someone else's perspective, thus helping you understand them. (For example, "Tell me more about that." "What is your opinion about _____?"). Come up with five statements or questions that you could use in almost any situation, and keep the list handy!
	37.	Learn to use reflective listening. Summarize the key thoughts and feelings of the others, but not by just repeating what they said. That can sound trivial. Instead, show them you understand by putting their message in your own words and indicating what emotion you heard. (For example, after a friend has told you he's really upset about a grade, you could say, "That's a bummer. You're really frustrated with that class and the grades you're getting in it.")

(continued)

	38.	Study others' facial expressions. Write down what you see. Bored? Interested? Concerned? Angry? Excited? Most emotional communication is nonverbal, so learning to scan others for nonverbal cues is important.
	39.	Solicit opinions from even the quietest group member. "Let's hear from someone who hasn't talked yet. We need to get all opinions out."
	40.	When interacting with one or more people about an issue or problem, make it a habit to ask at least three questions *before* you state your opinions or beliefs. Then show you have listened by briefly summarizing what you heard.
Social Responsibility	41.	Think of two or three things you can do to enhance a team's functioning—and then do them! The team could be a group project for a class, a sports team, a club, or any other group you belong to.
	42.	Call your team together and ask everyone to submit three to five ideas about how the team could function better as a unit. The team should then pick two or three ideas that seem most viable and workable and implement them.
	43.	Model a caring response. If, for example, someone at your school experiences a tragedy such as a house burning down, organize a collection of clothing and other needed items.
	44.	Stand up to bullies in your school by telling the bully to stop, inviting the victim to do things with you and your friends, or similar actions. If you stand up to a bully, others may also do so.
	45.	Get involved in your community through volunteer or service work.
	46.	Do simple things like take out the trash when it's full, empty the dishwasher without being asked, or other actions that show your cooperation.

Decision-Making Realm

Reality Testing	47.	Apply the A-E model (see Chapter 3) to situations in which you might exaggerate, catastrophize, jump to faulty conclusions, or overreact.
	48.	Practice distinguishing between facts (*I made a C on that paper*) and self-evaluations (*I'm a lousy writer*) and inferences (*That professor doesn't like me*). Stick with the facts and then take action to make changes!
	49.	The next time you have to make a big decision, write down three facts to support your conclusion (not three opinions, three inferences, or three ideas). If the decision is not based on at least three facts, keep searching for additional facts before making a decision.
	50.	Know your style! Do you tend toward overreaction (for example, exaggerating facts to get your point across, worrying about things beyond what is a typical or average reaction)? Or do you tend to underreact (for example, ignoring information that doesn't fit your plan, minimizing information that disagrees with your opinion, or failing to collect information because you don't want to have to change your course of action)? Once you have identified your style, identify a friend or family member with the opposite style. Before making important decisions, have a discussion with this person.
Problem Solving	51.	Analyze which of your triggered emotions are related to different types of problems. For example, do you become anxious about some types of assignments or some types of interpersonal conflict but not others? What types of problems trigger anger for you? Calm yourself down (deep breathing, exercise, meditation, taking a five-minute walk, and the like) before attempting to solve the problem.
	52.	Think of one very difficult problem you've encountered recently; write it down. Next, think of other issues that could be the root of the problem, rather than the surface problem. For example, suppose you are fighting a lot with your dating partner and you think the issue is about this person wanting to do things with friends more than you do. The real problem may be about different levels of commitment to the relationship. Identifying the real issue (root) will help you understand your emotions better. If you're stuck, ask others for their input about what the root problem may be.
	53.	Make sure to include others in idea generation as you try to problem solve issues that affect them. In other words, use a bottom-up approach, not a top-down approach to generate possible solutions.

(continued)

	54.	Generate several possible solutions for a problem and analyze the consequences of each before picking a solution.
	55.	After implementing a solution, collect data to determine whether the solution worked. If the data do not support an effective solution, repeat the steps of problem solving (correctly identify the issue, generate multiple ideas from people affected, choose, then implement.)
Impulse Control	56.	For anger issues: • Do not reply verbally, by text, or by email until you have calmed down. *If* you want to write the email or text, do so, just *don't send it*! • Use "I" messages and describe specific behaviors to explain to someone why you are mad. Avoid using harsh language, criticism, yelling, or punitive phrases. If you are really angry, write down the "I" message so you can deliver it effectively. • Take a walk to calm down before addressing the issue.
	57.	For lack of patience issues and impulse control issues: a. First identify whether your issues are related to eating (you overeat or eat unhealthy items too often), drinking (you over-consume), spending (you overcharge credit cards, overdraw your bank account, run up large amounts of debt), or time (you interrupt others with your points, work too quickly on tasks just to get them done, become overly irritated by waiting or traffic jams). Also identify whether there are certain circumstances that trigger this lack of impulse control (for example, overeating only when you're completing assignments). b. Now make environmental changes (for example, buy only healthy snack items at the grocery store, remove credit cards from your wallet, take a different route to school that may be more miles but has fewer traffic jams). c. Ask yourself one of two questions, depending on the type of impulse control situation encountered: (1) What is the worst that's going to happen because of this delay? (This works well for waiting in line and traffic jams.) (2) Do I really want to do this, even though I know the consequences? (This works well for impulsive spending, eating, drinking, and the like.)

Stress Management Realm

Flexibility	58. Change a routine (for example, what you do in the morning) that you feel very comfortable with; follow the changed routine until you adjust to it.
	59. Write down three to five technological changes that have occurred during your lifetime (for example, iPhone, Kindle, electric cars). Would your life be better without those changes? What can you learn about change from these examples?
	60. Identify at least two times in the last year that your opinion or course of action on an issue was changed *after* you received more information or talked with someone else about the issue. How did you adapt to that change?
	61. Know your style! Do you tend to hate change, fight it, and see it as a necessary evil? Or do you change quickly—perhaps too quickly—by flip-flopping your opinion with every new piece of information? Purposefully surround yourself with people who are different from you in this regard.
	62. Identify the most recent big change in your academic, work, or personal life. What specific strategies did you use to adapt to the change? Determine which ones helped you the most and the least, then incorporate the helpful strategies into all change situations.
Stress Tolerance	63. When working on academic tasks that create anxiety, take frequent breaks. Walk around outside or go to a favorite place and sit. Tune into how much you are reacting to the stressors of the work, and come up with one way to minimize one of the stressors.
	64. Pick a stress-relief activity, then engage in it at least five times a week: exercise, warm bath, massage, yoga, listening to music without doing any work, or whatever else relaxes you. Many things that people do for relaxation—such as video games—actually provide stimulation rather than relaxation.
	65. Keep a log of what you do when you are stressed. Do you overeat? Get irritable with others? Have trouble concentrating? Use your knowledge of your reactions to help you identify when stress has crept up on you.

(continued)

	66.	Make of list of "daily hassles" that stress you. Examples include bad traffic, a slow computer, and too much homework. Now list at least one way that you could: • Minimize your level of reaction to the stressor (let it bother you less). • Try to remove the stressor (for example, leave 10 minutes earlier to avoid traffic, or purchase more RAM for the computer).
Optimism	67.	Practice reframing situations from neutral or negative to positive. Here are some examples to help you! • A child from a family of 10 could relish the variety in clothes rather than being concerned about getting hand-me-downs. • A student who made a B instead of an A could view the experience as an opportunity to improve his or her work, rather than as a "bad grade." • A parent could choose to see crying as a form of communication from a baby rather than as a bother. • A principal could see lots of new people moving into the district as a positive endorsement of the school rather than as a space and hiring headache. • An athlete who doesn't start could view the opportunity to stand near the coach as a way to learn more about the game.
	68.	When confronted with a difficulty, make a list of what could go well.
	69.	Read some of the literature related to the benefits of optimism—everything from our reactions to illness to our academic performance.
	70.	Challenge your negative thoughts. For example, if you're taking physics for the first time, avoid thoughts such as "I've never done well in science." Instead, you could positively frame the situation as follows: "Physics involves a lot of math, more than biology, so I might do really well in physics because of my math background."
	71.	During adversity, develop a plan for how you are going to overcome the problem, then share it with others. Enlist their help, then persist until the issue is resolved effectively or no further intervention is possible.

A REVIEW OF SELF-TALK

Self-talk is a term for the messages we give ourselves while we are thinking about something. Those messages can be positive (for example, "I've done something like this before and really enjoyed it"), or they can be negative ("I've done something like this before and it didn't turn out well"). Both types of messages influence our reaction in the moment. Learning to practice positive and encouraging self-talk helps us perform more effectively. Self-talk can also be used as a reminder to do something (for example, "Ask two questions before stating my opinion"). And it can be used to help us slow down and analyze a situation (for example, "What could I do differently right now that might work out better? Am I doing anything to contribute to the problem?"). Develop a list of self-talk messages:

- Three or four *positive* self-talk messages
- Three or four *reminder* messages for how you want to act in certain situations
- Three or four *analysis* questions that will help you overcome difficult challenges

Think about times you will be likely to need your self-talk messages, and keep this list handy.

A REVIEW OF THE A-E MODEL

Cognitive psychologists like Ellis (2004) claim that rarely do events or situations cause our emotional responses; rather, it is our interpretations (beliefs) about the event and what it may mean for us that cause our reactions. For example, two students take the same cumulative organic chemistry test, but one has engaged in the irrational belief that "If I don't make an A in this course I will never get into medical school," whereas the other has engaged in positive self-talk such as "I've studied hard and have done well on the previous exams." The first student will perform worse on the test because the student's anxiety is so high that it will interfere with effective performance. Both students faced the same event (action), but their beliefs influence their different behaviors and emotional reactions. To review, here are the steps of the A-E model:

A = Action: Some event has occurred. (For example, your boss at work refuses to give you a weekend off.)

B = (irrational) Beliefs: We engage in irrational mental (self-talk) responses to the action. (For example, "My boss doesn't like me, so that's why she didn't give me the weekend off.")

C = Consequence: Irrational beliefs lead us to engage in behaviors that are premature, unjustified, or otherwise off base or show an overreaction. (For example, you may talk disparagingly about the boss to other workers or avoid interacting with the boss.) Irrational beliefs also cause fear, anxiety, anger, and other negative emotions.

D = Dispute: The best way to get rid of irrational beliefs is to dispute them with facts and evidence from past experiences. In this case, we might ask ourselves if our boss has ever said or done anything to indicate a dislike for us, what other people think about the boss (for example, do they think the boss is fair and friendly?), and whether there may be other reasons the boss refused to give you the weekend off (for example, it's a holiday weekend, you didn't ask for time off until three days before the weekend, or other factors).

E = (new) Effect: Once you have rationally challenged the irrational belief, it is easier to replace your behavior with more effective choices. (For example, you meet with your boss to find out how far ahead of time you have to request time off.) Also, your emotional responses will be less negative and you will remain calmer as you deal with the situation.

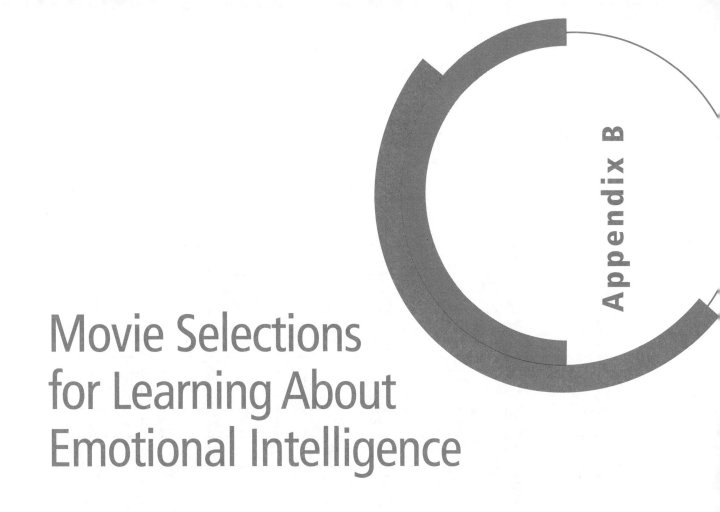

Movie Selections for Learning About Emotional Intelligence

Movie	Brief Description	Emotional Self-Awareness	Self-Regard	Self-Actualization	Emotional Expression	Independence	Assertiveness	Interpersonal Relationships	Empathy	Social Responsibility	Reality Testing	Problem Solving	Impulse Control	Flexibility	Stress Tolerance	Optimism	Happiness
12 Angry Men (not rated, drama)	A lone member of a jury slowly convinces the others of the defendant's innocence.					x	x		x		x				x		
All the President's Men (R, based on a true story, drama)	Two *Washington Post* reporters break the Watergate story, leading to Nixon's resignation.					x	x			x					x		
Avatar (PG-13, drama)	A marine is sent to carry out a mission to destroy a world he comes to love.	x	x	x	x	x		x	x	x							
Billy Elliot (PG-13, drama)	A young Irish boy discovers a love of dance despite objections from his family.	x		x	x	x										x	x
The Blind Side (PG-13, based on a true story)	A poor African-American boy is adopted by a family who helps him reach his potential.	x			x	x	x	x	x	x							

Title	Description															
Born Free (PG, based on a true story, drama)	A lion cub is adopted by a family but has to be taught to live in the wild as she matures.	x					x		x	x	x		x			
Catch Me If You Can (PG-13, based on a true story)	A young man commits financial crimes and escapes capture because of his intelligence.								x	x	x	x	x			
Coach Carter (PG-13, based on a true story)	A successful businessman takes over an unruly group of high school basketball players who resist his discipline.		x	x		x	x	x	x	x						
Cool Runnings (PG, drama, based on a true story)	A group of Jamaicans decide to enter the Olympics to compete in the bobsled event.		x	x		x	x	x	x	x		x	x			
The Devil Wears Prada (PG-13, comedy)	A critical boss terrorizes her staff until one employee stands up to her.					x	x				x					
Erin Brockovich (PG-13, drama, based on a true story)	A feisty single mother leads the effort to help residents of a small town fight a company that is poisoning their water.					x	x	x	x							
ET (PG, drama)	An extraterrestrial is adopted by children who help him hide from authorities eager to study him.	x				x	x		x	x	x			x		

(Continued)

Movie	Brief Description	Emotional Self-Awareness	Self-Regard	Self-Actualization	Emotional Expression	Independence	Assertiveness	Interpersonal Relationships	Empathy	Social Responsibility	Reality Testing	Problem Solving	Impulse Control	Flexibility	Stress Tolerance	Optimism	Happiness
The Family Stone (PG-13, comedy, drama)	A close-knit family rejects their son's fiancée, leaving him confused and her devastated.	X		X	X				X			X	X				X
A Few Good Men (R, drama)	A lawyer defends two marines accused of murder who were given the order by a commanding officer.		X			X	X		X				X				
Field of Dreams (PG, drama)	A man dreams of building a baseball field for baseball players accused of fixing games.	X		X												X	
Forrest Gump (PG-13, drama)	A mildly retarded young man lives a full life, yearning for a relationship with a childhood friend.		X		X	X	X	X	X							X	X
Georgia Rule (R, drama)	A rebellious teenager is sent to spend the summer with her strict grandmother.	X	X		X	X	X	X	X		X		X	X			X

Title																	
The Hunger Games (PG-13, drama) — A young woman challenges an oppressive government and risks her life and others'.	x		x		x		x			x	x	x	x	x			
My Big Fat Greek Wedding (PG, drama) — A woman needs to assert herself with her large and loving Greek family who interfere with her wedding plans.	x		x		x					x				x			x
My Sister's Keeper (PG-13, drama) — A young girl—who was conceived to provide a bone-marrow match for her sick sister—refuses any further medical procedures that would help her sister.	x		x		x					x				x			
Notting Hill (PG-13) — A famous actress connects with a bookstore owner but lets her fame interfere with the relationship.	x		x			x										x	x
The Odd Couple (comedy) — Two very different friends manage to share an apartment despite their differences.						x							x	x			
Odd Girl Out (PG-13, drama) — A teen girl is bullied by her friends because of her success and popularity.	x		x		x		x	x	x	x	x	x	x	x	x	x	x
One Fine Day (PG, comedy) — Two busy single parents share child-care responsibility when they both have big days scheduled at work.	x		x		x		x	x	x	x	x	x	x	x			

(Continued)

Movie	Brief Description	Emotional Self-Awareness	Self-Regard	Self-Actualization	Emotional Expression	Independence	Assertiveness	Interpersonal Relationships	Empathy	Social Responsibility	Reality Testing	Problem Solving	Impulse Control	Flexibility	Stress Tolerance	Optimism	Happiness
Patch Adams (PG-13, based on a true story, comedy)	An irreverent middle-aged man attends med school, rocking the health care establishment with his unconventional ways of helping the sick.	x	x	x	x	x	x	x	x	x	x	x				x	x
Pay It Forward (PG-13, drama)	A young boy teaches others to "pay back" kindness by "paying it forward" to someone in need.			x					x	x		x				x	x
The Pursuit of Happyness (PG-13, based on a true story, drama)	A single parent, homeless father struggles to care for his son while he works to land a job with a major corporation.		x	x				x				x		x	x	x	x
Remember the Titans (PG, based on a true story, drama)	A coach takes over a racially divided football team and teaches them to work together and care for each other.		x				x			x		x	x			x	

The Rookie (G, based on a true story, drama)	A high school baseball coach takes on the challenge from his team to try out for a pro team; he makes it to the big leagues, only to question his decision.	X	X	X				X						X
Runaway Bride (PG-13, comedy)	A woman scared of marriage keeps running away from her wedding ceremonies.	X						X		X			X	
Schindler's List (R, based on a true story, drama)	A German factory owner helps Jews evade the Nazi death camps.						X	X	X					
School Ties (PG-13, drama)	A working-class Jewish high school senior tries to hide his religion while living amid conservative classmates at an elite private school; they accuse him of cheating to get him expelled.					X	X			X	X			
Sister Act (PG, comedy)	A nightclub singer takes up residence in a convent to escape the mob and has to adapt her behavior to her new life.			X			X	X			X	X		

(Continued)

Movie	Brief Description	Emotional Self-Awareness	Self-Regard	Self-Actualization	Emotional Expression	Independence	Assertiveness	Interpersonal Relationships	Empathy	Social Responsibility	Reality Testing	Problem Solving	Impulse Control	Flexibility	Stress Tolerance	Optimism	Happiness
To Kill a Mockingbird (drama, not rated)	A white lawyer defends an obviously innocent black man falsely accused of rape in the 1930s south.						x	x					x				
What About Bob? (PG, comedy)	A clingy patient follows his psychiatrist on a vacation and makes friends with his family, sending the psychiatrist to the brink of his own collapse.				x			x				x	x		x	x	x
What Women Want (PG-13, comedy)	A chauvinist male is passed over for promotion and has to report to a female boss; suddenly he can hear everything women are thinking, giving him a new outlook.	x	x					x	x					x			
You've Got Mail (PG, comedy)	A bookstore owner unknowingly connects online to the large book chain owner about to shut down her business.	x	x		x						x						x